Spirit to Spirit

Spirit to Spirit

**Poems and Prose
Stories and Thoughts
From Friends at Holy Spirit Lutheran
Kirkland, Wa.**

Introduction by Pastor Larry Morris

**Contributors include:
Patricia Anderson, Beverly Berg, Minna Brask, Otto Brask,
Kim Deskin, Clara Hanley, Ruth Hanley, Pat Mason,
Pastor Katy McCallum Sachse, Pastor Larry Morris,
Suzanne Morris, Marlene Obie, Dave Patneaude,
RuthAnn Wilson**

*Illustrations by Lyla Jacobsen
Cover Photo by Ross Taylor*

*Editing and Cover design by
Larry Morris*

Copyright © 2011 Larry Morris

All rights reserved.

All contributors to this book have given rights for the use of their material in this book only. Any further use of their material needs to have the individual author's specific permission.

ISBN-13:978-1466347618
ISBN-10:1466347619

For additional copies check on Amazon.com or contact Larry Morris at PLarryMorris@Gmail.com

Contents

1. Thoughts on Faith 1

- **Drink Deeply** 2
  - by Pastor Larry Morris 2
- **Deliverance in The Desert** 4
  - by RuthAnn Wilson... 4
- **Easter, Once Again!** 7
  - by Otto Brask... 7
- **Religious Experience** 8
  - by Kim Deskin 8
- **Same Old Story** 10
  - by Kim Deskin 10
- **We are the Girls** 11
  - by Clara Hanley 11
- **Happy Feet**..14
  - by RuthAnn Wilson... 14
- **Thank You Jesus** 16
  - by Beverly Berg 16
- **Step by Step** 18
  - by Marlene Obie... 18
- **Spring** 19
  - by Suzanne Morris.. 19
- **Qualities of Grass** 20
  - by Suzanne Morris.. 20
- **Congo Christmas** 22
  - by RuthAnn Wilson... 22
- **Holding Hope in My Hand** 24
  - by RuthAnn Wilson... 24
- **The Image of God** 26

by Pastor Larry Morris 26
The Eyes Of Christ! 28
   by RuthAnn Wilson 28
Remember, You are Dust 30
   by Larry Morris 30
Whispers From The Black Hole 31
   by RuthAnn Wilson 31

2. Life and Love Stories 35

Me Do It 36
   by RuthAnn Wilson 36
My Father's Hat 38
   by Beverly Berg 38
Thank You Robinson Crusoe 41
   by Beverly Berg 41
Valentine's Day 45
   by Beverly Berg 45
Those Tears 48
   by Marlene Obie 48
Fields of Earth, Field of Love 49
   by Pastor Larry Morris 49

3. Wisdom in Words 51

Shoreline 52
   by Pat Mason 52
February 53
   by Pat Mason 53
Creatrix 54
   by Ruth Hanley 54
Little Ivy Thoughts 55
   by Marlene Obie 55
Thankful for Living 56
   by Suzanne Morris 56
Self! Shut Up Your Murmuring! 57
   by Marlene Obie 57
Never Walk Alone. 58
   by Otto Brask 58

Three Baby Banty Chicks 60
   by RuthAnn Wilson 60
Water 63
   by Pat Mason 63
Listening to the Thunder 64
   by Kim Deskin 64
Time Trials 66
   by Marlene Obie 66
Attitude 68
   by Marlene Obie 68
The Preacher's Ballet Slippers 69
   By Pastor Larry Morris 70
Negativity 72
   by Marlene Obie 72

4. Just for Fun 75
The Problem with Easter 76
   by Ruth Hanley 76
The Effect of Alcohol 77
   by Minna Brask 77
A Ghost Story 78
   by Minna Brask 78
Big Old House on the Corner 80
   by Pastor Larry Morris 80

5. On Friendship and Family 83
On My Way to the Sudoku 84
   by David Patneaude 84
Co-Sleeper's Neck 86
   by Ruth Hanley 86
Gourmand 87
   by Ruth Hanley 87
"Berries? Go Berries?" 88
   by RuthAnn Wilson 88
Song To My Friend 91
   by RuthAnn Wilson 91
Thirty Two Tiny Valentines 92

    by Pastor Larry Morris 92
In the Midst of Darkness **94**
    by Pastor Larry Morris 94
6. Short Stories and a Sermon 97
The Family Auction **98**
    by Patricia Anderson 98
Christmas Eve Sermon **101**
    by Pastor Katy McCallum Sachse 101
The Trouble with God **106**
    by **Beverly** Berg 106
INDEX of Author's Names, First Lines and illustrations .. 118

INTRODUCTION

In the summer of 2009, I advertised that we would be having a meeting of artists and writers in our congregation, to discuss the possibility of holding a congregational Art and Literature Show. My advertisement encouraged people to bring a piece of their work to show us.

Although I knew we had at least a few people with artistic talent in the congregation, I had no idea who would be interested or how many would come. Fourteen people showed up and shared with the rest of us, one of their creations and, with it, a part of their heart.

In the two years since then, we have had two shows which have included oil paintings, watercolors, photography, carvings, sculptures, a handmade doll and rocker, computer animation, lapidary, needle-point, quilts, decorated boxes, lots of writing and much more.

Out of the first show, a writing group was formed as a way to encourage each other to write and to create a place to share and read what we have written. If the author is open to suggestions, we share them, but mostly we encourage each other to write! Sometimes the encouragement comes in the form of laughter or tears, other times oooh's and ahhhh's.

At the shows, one of the familiar comments we received about the literature was that people wanted to be able to sit with the writings and a cup of coffee and have time to experience them - rather than stand and read them as they were posted on a wall. Out of those comments and the realization that we were continuing to write - the idea of a book was born!

The writings, cover picture and sketches included in this book are all by members and friends of the congregation.

As we collected writings someone suggested we include simple pictures to go along with the writings – to make the book for visually appealing. We asked Lyla Jacobsen, an artist in the congregation, if she would take on the task. She took our request seriously and created beautiful watercolors and oil paintings that captured the heart of ten of the written pieces! Wonderful!

We asked Ross Taylor, another member of our congregation, if he had or could take a photograph that would work for the cover. As we brainstormed he mentioned he had taken pictures of our stained glass windows. We used a piece of one of those pictures for the cover. It fits the title and ties us to our faith home, Holy Spirit Lutheran. Perfect!

There are writings in this book from people we knew were good communicators, along with writings from people whose skills used to be hidden! Hidden no more!

Thank you to all of the authors and artists who participated in this work. Your work and creativity inspires me. Keep writing, painting and photographing!

Thank you to Marlene Obie and Ross Taylor our meticulous proof readers who performed a detailed, significant and tedious work! Thank you to Ross for many of the portraits of the Authors and Artists! And thank you to Kristen Lloyd for creating the bookmark that went with the first printing!

Finally thank you to you, our readers. These works are intended for your enjoyment, your inspiration and some of them were written 'just for your fun'!

Happy Reading!
Pastor Larry Morris

p.s. Additional thanks to Karen Dicken who helped figure out how we were going to distribute this book and to my good friend John Boose, whose instructions on formatting and enthusiastic encouragement saved this project more than once!

Authors' and Artists' Biographies

Patricia Anderson was raised on a farm in southern Minnesota. She graduated from the University of Minnesota and has spent most of her career as a nurse. Patty especially enjoys reading pioneer stories and admires pioneer women and the hardships they endured. Patty lives in Kirkland Washington with her husband Pastor Michael Anderson and daughter Sara.

Beverly Berg – "Once upon a time there was a depression in our country. I experienced it; that's why I write about it" When not writing, Beverly has been a mother, grandmother, story teller, actress, sheep herder, rattlesnake shooter, P-53 riveter, prison teacher and those are only the things she was been willing to tell us about so far!

Minna Brask - Born in Denmark, USA is my second country. I came to Seattle in 1961 as an exchange nurse at Swedish Hospital, hoping to go back and take a degree in nursing. I met my husband here, and we married in 1962, which ended my ambitions to continue my nursing career. For many years I have been writing to a Danish newspaper printed in Los Angeles and written many small anecdotes. I have also worked as an RN at Kirkland Hospital and on private cases.

Otto Brask - I was born and grew up in Denmark. In 1953, I immigrated to the United States, and have resided in the Seattle area since 1959. I am a machinist, retired from University of Washington since 1992. I am an amateur wood worker, and I dabble in vegetable gardening, long-time member of Holy Spirit Lutheran Church and a frequent visitor to Holden Village.

Kim Deskin reveals yet another hidden talent with the publication of her poetry. The known list: parent, teacher, actor, director, cook, small-group leader, composition coach, service project coordinator, and all around nice person.

Clara Hanley is 5 years old and sometimes expresses herself in poetic form when least expected. The following poem is one that she told her mommy. Poetry can be a tool for children to express themselves past what they can consciously communicate at a young age and it is amazing to get a glimpse into their young minds.

Ruth Hanley is a monkey-tamer, bomb-diffuser, plate-spinner, short order cook at a carnival and a witch doctor who offers ice packs for hurt feelings. I have two girls, a 5-year-old who's a Drama Queen that likes M&M Blizzards and a 1 1/2 year old who is able to get to the top of the refrigerator with your matches, cell phone and a popsicle if you turn your eyes away for 1 second. I have been married to my Prince Charming for about 10 years and find that the answer to most problems around here is either kisses &/or cheerios and am working on a way to apply this to the rest of the world.

Lyla Jacobsen is an Eastside artist, mostly working in oils and is represented by Kaewyn Gallery, Kirkland Art Center, and Candler Gallery in Alberta. Her paintings are of scenes or subjects that suddenly catch her eye, be it landscape, seascape, commonplace items about her home, or moments that tell a story.

Pastor Katy McCallum Sachse serves at Holy Spirit Lutheran Church in Kirkland. She and her husband Brian are the parents of one delightful daughter and spend most of their free time baby proofing the house.

Pastor Larry Morris. I am a CFO, Pastor, husband, father, biker, chicken wrangler, piano beginner, cook, pray-er, water-color painter, wood carver and writer. Watch for my first book in the spring of 2012!

Pat Mason and her husband are parents of three wonderful daughters and a 'beginning to be' spoiled grandson! Writing has been a meaningful and mostly private hobby. "To read, to write.....it's a vital medium for those of us who find speech inadequate."

Suzanne Morris – Sharing with you is a blast, some poetry from my past. I have enjoyed writing poetry and prose since my 20s. I have always loved God's creation!
I am a psychotherapist in private practice. I believe in helping people change in the least stressful way for their body, mind and soul. You can learn more about what I do at www.counselnheal.com

Marlene Obie - Septuagenarian author of 2 books, articles, devotions, blog (marlenesmusings.com) and prayers harvested out of life's ever-changing revelations and surprises. Children, grandchildren, pastors, church families, friends and the Grace of God are gifts that make my days. Read Marlene's blog " http://www.marlenesmusings.com/"

David Patneaude - "I like the outdoors, sports, travel, movies, and plays, and when I want to take a quiet break from my writing, I still enjoy indulging one of my first loves: reading." David has published a number of award winning books for middle-school aged kids. His latest book is **_Epitaph Road_**. His Website is http://www.patneaude.com

Ross Taylor is a retired dentist who has taken up photography with passion and great joy. He understands his photographic art with the mind of a professional and the heart of an artist

RuthAnn Wilson. I am a life-long Lutheran, and have attended HSLC since I moved to Kirkland in 2008. My hobbies include reading, traveling, gardening, genealogy, writing, and sometimes painting. I have 4 adult children and 13 grandchildren. Prior to my retirement, I taught pre-school through college in the public school systems in Washington, Pennsylvania, and the International School Service in Africa; I also taught summer programs on 6 continents. Since I retired from teaching, I spend about 5 months a year reconnecting to my roots in Wisconsin, where I volunteer at Norskedalen Nature and Heritage Center.

1. Thoughts on Faith

Drink Deeply
by Pastor Larry Morris

The water runs over the head
and back into the font.
"I baptize you…".
In that water
and in those words
love touches us.
The invisible become visible,
the intangible becomes tangible ,
the universal becomes personal
"for you".
Life is renewed.
We are born a second time,
we are re-created.

Then the water returns to its work.
It runs into our drains
and into our streams,
into our rivers
and into the
lakes.
It evaporates
into our clouds
and gathers into
our rain.
It gives life to
the plants of the
field
and fish in the
sea,
the birds of the
air
and to us.

It renews
and refreshes.
It quenches
and gives life.
It comes and it goes
again and again.

Where has this water been
that sits in this cup in front of me?
Was it at the beginning
when God separated
the dry land from the seas?
Was it there
when Moses parted the waters?
Was it there when Jesus
was baptized?
Was it there
when I was baptized?
Now it sits here
in front of me.

This water of life,
come again
and again,
is calling me to remember
God's creation in the beginning
and God's re-creation
in me
and in you.

Drink Deeply

Deliverance in The Desert
by RuthAnn Wilson

I love to travel! I love the adventure, the fun, the beauty, and even the challenge of the unknown! One June I planned a drive through the springtime beauty of the desert to visit my friends Sandy and Madeline in Tulsa, Oklahoma.

On a glorious morning, Sandy suggested we all go for a drive to visit their friends about 40 miles out of town. After an early brunch, the five of us climbed into their van and headed west. The scenic drive was notable for the gorgeous but desolate desert. The earth radiated heat waves, and I was fascinated by the strange beauty of the dry, barren landscape.

There was very little traffic. After about 30 miles, we pulled off the highway onto a narrow country road. Ten miles later we arrived at their friend's home. We had an enjoyable visit, sipped iced tea, and relaxed in their rustic rural home.

Late in the afternoon, it was time to start the drive back to Tulsa. We drove the ten miles back to the highway slowly, deep in conversation. When the tires reached the smooth highway, we turned toward Tulsa. Suddenly, the van lost power and Sandy coasted the van to a stop. She said, "Guess what, folks? We're out of gas!"

Startled into silence, we

Realized our afternoon drive had become a little scary. What if we were stranded way out here? Those clouds in the west looked dark and threatening. We looked around for a gas station, but saw only flat sand and sagebrush. We were stopped on a highway with absolutely no building in sight, and not a car on the highway. As far as we could see, there was no sign of life.

Together, we wondered which direction would be the closest for finding a gas station. How far would we have to walk? I privately worried about how quickly night would come out here in the desert, and what about those clouds? As we got out of the car, Sandy took charge and decided two of us should walk west and the other two east, with one person staying by the car.

After taking about three steps, I had a strong urge to pray. I said to the others, "Let's pray together before we do anything."

Madeline said, "Let's pray it won't take long to find gas!"

Sandy said, "Maybe somebody will come along and give us a ride."

Then I said, "Let's pray someone comes along and gives us gas!"

I felt a little foolish making such a bold statement. Everybody laughed. But we joined our hands together and prayed that God would send help.

Then we turned to walk for help. After five minutes, a dust cloud appeared, coming toward us from the west. As it came near, we could see a dusty green pick-up truck towing a boat. The driver began to slow to a stop.

He got out and asked if we needed help. We explained that we were out of gas. He said, "Well, I just happen to have an extra five-gallon can of gas in the boat. Let's put it in your van!"

He refused to take any money for it, and drove off with a smile. We waved goodbye, and Sandy started the van's engine. As we headed home, the beauty of the desert once again emerged as the sun drove away the clouds.

Easter, Once Again!
by Otto Brask

On a sunny day, a few days before Easter about ten years ago, I stopped by the Strictly Scandinavian store in Gig Harbor. The store-owner, Inge Miller, a fellow Dane, and her husband Jim, have been friends of ours for many years. We met them first time on a summer's visit to Holden Village years ago.

It was a lovely warm spring day, flowers in bloom all around, the world seemed at peace. Just then, as we talked in the doorway of her store, the bells from the tower of the Baptist Church across the parking lot intoned a familiar hymn: "Were you there, when they crucified my Lord?" Crisp and clear the message of Good Friday and Easter rang out over the little town and busy waterfront for everyone to hear. We were both moved and listened quietly through the first stanza and then hummed along, not quite sure of the rest of the words, but remembering the lines: -- "sometimes it causes me to tremble. Were you there, when they crucified my Lord?"
For a short while, it almost seemed like a communion. Having similar backgrounds and being on the same Christian wavelength, we shared a few precious moments. We seemed to know each other's thoughts.

As we said our Good-byes, speaking mostly Danish, we wished each other God Påske, the Danish for Happy Easter.

Religious Experience
by Kim Deskin

Easter morning, we all go to church.
    (My husband's family is Catholic, you know.)
I sit in the cry room with my son;
They—and the other thousand—line the walls in the sanctuary.
    (We always run late, you know.)
I'm lonely and miserable, squished between parents
    I won't see again for eight months or so.

I think: I don't have to be here.
    (That obligation thing you know.) I don't have to,
So, we leave.

I take my son outside and we sit on the porch step.
We enjoy the sunshine and comfortable breeze.
I describe for him God's love for us.
I sing along with a song I kind of recognize.
I love my son. I love the day. Everything is beautiful.

Then, I see a priest, heading in to commune.
    (He'll probably scold me, you know.)
    (He'll probably damn me, you know.)
I panic. I look for a way to hide. But, of course,
    there is no place to hide.
At least, I'll avoid his glare.
    (If he can't see me, I'm not here, right?)

I can't help but acknowledge him. I mutter hello.

He lightly touches my son's head, then my shoulder,
    as he passes. A genuine blessing. And he says,
    "You've got the idea. You've got the idea."

Same Old Story
by Kim Deskin

There was a man—
    a young man—
travelling across the country
    "to find himself."

He grew weary on the journey,
    not of the external trip
        for the country can be beautiful,
    but of the internal quest
        for oneself is always hard to find.

He asked for a sign—
    some token,
        just for him,
    in the next five minutes.

He drove. He watched. He drove.
He stopped for coffee. He drove.

Later that night
    he passed a fire—
    a brush fire that had
        by that point dwindled down
        to one smoldering bush.
A woman stood next to the bush
and turned to the passing truck.

The man glanced at his watch
    and drove on.

    Five minutes had passed hours ago.

We are the Girls
    by Clara Hanley

We are the girls
   who sing everywhere
      we hear al-le-luias in the air!

My Childhood prayer:
by Ruth Hanley

'Now I lay me down to sleep'
Well, I'm not really going to sleep – I told Mom I was afraid
of the dark so that I could read by the hall light shining
through the open door – is that a lie? Lying is a sin. I'm not off
to a good start...
'I pray the Lord my soul to keep'
Um...I see my soul as sort of Peter Pan's shadow, stuck to the
tip of my toe. Can you take that away? Why do I have to pray
to keep it?
'If I should die'
DIE???
'Before I wake'
Maybe I'd better get a few more books so I can stay
awake...this is gonna be a long night.
'I pray the Lord my soul to take.'
What if he forgets? Or what if I forget to pray this part – will
he still take it? What if the devil makes me say "I DON'T want
you to take it – even though I do. What does a soul even look
like that God can "take" it? Where does he take them? Aaaah!!
'If I should live another day...'
IF???
'I pray the Lord to guide my ways'
What happens if I mess up?
[then quickly name everyone you know or are related to so that
they don't die – if they do, it will be all your fault]

Night time prayer that I share with my children:
'Now I lay me down to sleep

I pray the Lord my soul to keep
Let angels guide me through the night
And wake me with the morning light.'
Aaah…angels. God is hugging my soul while Angels are guiding me to the morning and waking me up, refreshed. I hope that this is how the kids perceive this as well though. What if this was the intent with the original version of this prayer – the one that filled me with fear, trepidation and brought out an obsessive-compulsive disorder each night?
'Now, who do you want to bless tonight? A blessing is when God holds someone's hand that needs it. Who needs a special hand-holding from God? What are you thankful for? What else do you want to talk to God about?'
[Then listen to anything my kids are upset about or thinking about or happy about until it's lullaby time.]

A Mother's Prayer:
'God, please guide me through this prayer and give me answers if they're there.
If there's no answer to be found, let them see your love abound'

Happy Feet
by RuthAnn Wilson

"Oh, no! Tami! I forgot to bring my sandals! I have only these heavy winter shoes!"

We spent the previous night at the airport hotel, planning to catch an early flight to Mexico on a cold winter morning in Seattle.

"Mom! How could you forget sandals?"

"I had them sitting right by the door. But I guess as we left the house I just put on these winter shoes."

"Oh, Mom,' Tami consoled me, "you can get new ones when we get to Puerto Vallarta."

"Most people could, I guess. But my feet are so hard to fit, and I am just miserable if my feet don't feel good."

"I understand, Mom." Tami reached out and gave me a hug, then stood back with her hand still on my arm.

She closed her eyes and prayed, "Jesus, we need you here right now. My Mom needs Happy Feet if we are to have a good trip to Mexico. Please find shoes that will fit her and show us where they are. Amen."

My stress instantly drained away. I looked at Tami in surprise, as she seldom prays aloud. "Thank you, Tami. It's going to be OK now."

Hours later, after checking into our hotel room in Puerto Vallarta, we decided to walk to a grocery store and get some munchies. The sun was shining, and we were delighted with the warm weather. I didn't say anything as we strolled down the street, but I was still feeling embarrassed about wearing the clunky black shoes.

Five minutes later we opened the door to the air-conditioned grocery store. The first thing inside the door was a tall revolving shoe rack covered with Crocs of all sizes.

"Mom, look! Let's see if these are your new shoes!"

"At a grocery store! I can't possibly find shoes that fit me at a grocery store, Tami."

I glanced at the rack again. Many colors of these funny-looking shoes were arrayed up and down the rack. I reached for a pair of white ones. "These are so ugly! But I did see lots of people wearing them last summer."

The first pair I picked up was marked with my size. "Wow! I usually have a hard time finding my size – look, Tami! This is my size right here!"

"Mom, try them on. They are going to fit you just perfectly. You are going to have Happy Feet."

I slipped my feet into both Crocs, stood up straight, took several steps, and exclaimed in amazement, "Tami! You are so right. These fit perfectly. Oh, they are wonderful! Will you try some on, too?"

Tami already had a pair of Crocs in her hand, and she slipped them onto her feet. We felt like we were walking on heavenly clouds, as we thanked God for answered prayer and for giving us both Happy Feet.

Thank You Jesus
by Beverly Berg

The four of us, my older sister Jean, younger brother and sister, Neil and Lorraine, and I, Beverly, had made it to our country school this morning. But the snow had been deep, and it was hard walking, especially for three miles.

Our teacher, Miss Grace, had a warm fire going in the potbelly stove.

"Are you worried about the weather?" Miss Grace asked as she saw me looking out of the window.

"I'm a little worried," I said, "because it's starting to snow, and these North Dakota badlands are tough to walk through, especially during a blizzard."

We saluted the flag, but instead of opening our books we all went to the windows. It had started to snow harder and there was a small wind starting to blow.

"I don't like the looks of the sky," I said. "And if the wind blows any harder, we're in for a blizzard."

Miss Grace said, "I think you'd better put your coats back on and start for home now."

We were about a mile from school when the blizzard hit. We couldn't see a thing when the snow hit our faces. We stopped and fastened our scarves to each other. Our younger sister Lorraine, was at the end of the line and could no longer make it through the deep snow and strong wind.

"I'm really afraid," I said to my sister Jean. "I don't know what to do. We can't let Lorraine lie down. She'll freeze."

Suddenly, I knew how I could find an answer. I looked up into the falling snow and prayed. "Lord Jesus, please, please help us."

I waited and hoped. Then, the answer came. "Dig a cave."

"Hey, Neil and Jean, we have to dig a cave in the highest snowdrift we can find. I can't see a thing, but maybe we can feel."

"I found one," Neil yelled, "and it's just right for digging. Remember that warm day we had three days ago? The snow is just right. Let's dig a hole first to put Lorraine in, out of the blizzard."

When we placed her in the hole, we all took off our scarves to cover her. Then the three of us started to dig. Our six hands and arms worked quickly, and we soon had a fairly large tunnel. When we were protected from the blizzard, we could work even faster.

We agreed that the size would hold the four of us, so we lifted our sleeping sister from her hole and placed her in the back of the cave.

"Wake up! Wake up! Move your arms and legs," I said as we all settled in. "Let's all try to keep moving. I'll sing. You keep time."

We waited. It seemed for hours.

"Thank you Jesus," I whispered.

Then, suddenly, I thought I heard dogs barking. I crawled out of the cave into the blinding snow and began to yell. Jean and Neil followed, and we hoped that three people yelling would be heard above the blizzard.

"Please, Jesus, please," I whispered.

And we were heard! Suddenly, there was a team and sleigh right in front of us. Tippy and Rover were on their hind legs licking our cheeks. Mom was crying. Dad was carrying Lorraine to the sleigh. As Jean, Neil and I lay on the hay on the bottom of the wagon, Mom covered us with heavy woolen blankets.

I looked up toward the sky, and with tears running down my cheeks. I whispered, "Thank you Jesus."

Step by Step
by Marlene Obie

Dear God, my daily guide throughout my life,

Thank you for showing me safe steps as I walk down the slick rock of canyon walls and climb back up. Help my hold of trust to remain steady as I watch and place my feet in your indentations.

Keep my eyes on your faithful, experienced path, and not over the edge, lest I lose my balance to fear. Show me, dear Lord the highest good to follow.

Forgive me for wandering off in search of pastures which seem to be promising fodder, but leave my quest for fulfillment unsatisfied. Keep me focused on the abundance of your continuing love that contains all the genuine sustenance I need.

I pray for daily restoration and acceptance of who I am, your beloved emissary, endowed with power to get through thorny brush, negotiate switchbacks and stay upright on slippery, loose surfaces. Shut out from my ears the chattering lies of deceivers, within and outside of myself, who would convince my will that I won't. Hold my faith and head up and keep my foot steady and on course.

I pray for Grace, Lord, for the love which covers my doubts and stretches me out.
I believe you will always lead me in your foresight and I will follow:
Step by step;
Moment by moment;.
Prayer by prayer.

Spring
by Suzanne Morris

The sound of a plane overhead
A chirp of a baby bird
The smell of the flowers
Wafting through the air

A gentle, cool breeze
Rustling the trees
The sun warming the earth
Feeding the countryside

Spring moves across the land
Laying her gentle green fingers
On the tiniest of plants
To the tallest of trees

Transforming all into lush greens
With a touch of pink or blue
Of lovely flowers
Peeking through

A peacefulness lies on the land
Of new birth
Young…
Tender…

Calming the spirit
As it moves around and through all
Knowing all is well
God is present

Qualities of Grass
by Suzanne Morris

There are qualities in a blade of grass
I would certainly like to own

To be so bright and cheery
Having so little to possess

Using only what it needs
From the environment around it

Not to demand things for itself
Knowing it does not need them

Appearing so content
Just to be itself

Not trying to be something else
That it would find difficult to be

Taking everything in stride
So accepting of it all

Able to spring back so easily
After it has been stepped on

To offer itself as a cushion
A comfort to a weary soul

Loving the warmth of the sun
Like I love the warmth of God's love

Growing, nourished by it
Like I am with God's wisdom

God created this world
And all the things in it

Yes, even a blade of grass
And the qualities it possesses

Congo Christmas
by RuthAnn Wilson

Stars
In the heavens -
Different constellations
Here at the Equator of Africa.
The sheep and goats look somewhat the same;
The yearning of the heart is very much the same.
Is a Savior coming? Is there mercy, forgiveness, peace?
Is there a cup of water or a bite of bread?
Can you hear the voice crying in the wilderness?
I'm looking out my window at glorious flowering summertime,
Savoring fresh ocean breezes blowing through tropical palms.
I'm hearing the sounds of Africa: voices, laughter, sobbing,
and song.
All who dwell in the Northern Hemisphere
Experience wintry climes as they anticipate Christmas.
But here in the hot, and humid rainforest of Equatorial Africa,
Christmas comes with less fanfare of the seasons. Christmas
does come, nevertheless,
Because Christmas is not a matter of seasons or snow or
shopping malls;
Christmas happens in the manger of the heart.
It may seem strange, it does seem strange, that here in Pointe
Noire,
In the deepest darkest Congo, in the heart of Africa,
I feel the joy and the presence of the Christ.
I pray that you will know
His Coming in your heart.

My life-changing year in Africa taught me much about love, trusting God, learning to live unafraid. The first months were very difficult - at that time there was no way to stay in touch with folks at home except through writing letters, sometimes taking months to be received. That lack of communication from home heightened my perceptions and adjustment to being fully 'there'. Every time I walked outside my own rooms, I saw heartbreaking conditions: sickness, poverty, neglect, hopelessness, fear. But I also became acquainted with folks who showed me the richest hospitality I have ever experienced, showed me a living faith as they invited me to worship with them. I admit that I often returned to my home crying "Lord, what do you want me to do?" As Christmas approached, I felt lonely and heartsick and wrote this poem. RuthAnn Wilson 1992

Holding Hope in My Hand
by RuthAnn Wilson

Arriving home after a long day, I saw the blinking light on the phone as I opened the door. Shrugging off my coat, I pushed the button and heard Mom's voice: "Please come over as soon as you can. Nicky died this afternoon and we buried him at the back of the garden. Daddy is feeling terribly sad. I hope you can help him feel better."

Mom's message slammed into my brain as my heart raced erratically. "Oh, no," I thought to myself, "Dad can't take losing his dog now."

Faithful Nicky had been by Daddy's side herding dairy cows on the farm, and later sat with him through open-heart surgery and recovery. Now that Daddy's macular degeneration had robbed him of his vision, Nicky was more important than ever.

What could I say that would ease Dad's pain?
What words could console Dad in this grief? How could I give comfort when my own sense of peace and trust in God's presence was feeling so bruised?

I knew I couldn't face driving over to my parent's home until after I walked and prayed. Throwing my coat back on and grabbing some tissues, I walked the quarter mile through the dusk to my friend Diane's house.

With hot tears running down my face, I could barely see where I was walking. My thoughts cried out, "Oh, God, why did Nicky have to die? What can I say to comfort Daddy? Dear God, please help me find the words to say."

I walked up the steps of Diane's front porch and rang her doorbell. As I waited, my heart began to calm down, and I wiped the tears from my face. Then cleaning the streaks from my glasses, I turned and looked up.

The porch light focused on a single blossom of bright fuchsia hanging from a planter near my head. I gently reached out and touched the blossom with my fingertip, and then cupped it in my hand.

Stunned by the miniscule perfection of this one single bloom, I stood amazed. Each tiny fold of the blossom was perfect; each petal was flawless. Somehow I suddenly felt as if I held the Universe in my palm.

The unblemished beauty reminded me of Psalms 50:2, "Out of Zion, the perfection of beauty, God shines forth." Out of the purity and perfection of this little flower, God's Spirit comforted my heart with assurance that God was still at work, making all things right.

As I looked up in thanksgiving, the evening star winked back at me with a message of peace and hope. I would have the words my Dad needed to hear.

The Image of God
by Pastor Larry Morris

She had been a pastor,
a Holy Woman,
for 23 years.
She had served three congregations
and loved them all.

People knew
that she saw in them
the image of God.
She saw it as she
worked with them
laughed with them
confronted them
comforted them
and grew old with them.

She never put them down,
or made fun of them
for the things they lacked
or for the fears they carried.
She saw in everyone
the image of God
and she called it forth
with great honor
and profound wisdom.
Her people were blessed
and changed
by her vision.

In retirement
she has taken up
painting portraits.

In the image of God
she paints them.
Male and Female
she paints them.

"Ohhhh" people say
as they see
her vision.

"Wow" they say
to the image of God.

"Yes" they say
as they see each other
with new eyes.
"Yes"

The Eyes Of Christ!
by RuthAnn Wilson

As my hand reached for the bread, my Pastor repeated Christ's words, "given for you". I dipped the bread in the wine as he said, "...shed for you and for all people..." I chewed, I swallowed, I made the sign of the cross, and then I reached for the chalice of wine.

It was my first time to assist with serving Holy Communion. It was also a special occasion celebrating All Saints Day with four other congregations. Standing together at the front of the church with my pastor, I remembered the words of my catechism instruction: "In, with, and under the consecrated bread and wine, Christ himself is truly and really present."

Turning to face the congregation, I saw the long line of people begin coming forward. Suddenly, I felt awestruck and overwhelmed by the sacredness of what we were about to do.
One by one, people appeared before me with outstretched hands holding consecrated bread. As each one dipped bread into the chalice, I spoke, "The Blood of Christ, shed for you." Eyes met mine as I heard a quiet "Amen." Over and over again, hands reached, eyes met, and a quiet "Amen" was breathed.

My eyes met the eyes of others: blue eyes, brown eyes, young and innocent eyes, watery old eyes. One by one, one after another, I continued to repeat the words, "The Blood of Christ, shed for you." As each one reached, chewed, swallowed, I saw them one by one, by the dozens, by the hundreds, as my lips continued to repeat the words "... shed for you." I caught my breath, as I began to sense a miraculous transformation – it was as if Christ was looking back at me through the eyes of each one.

I was filled with amazed awe at what God was doing, how God was present. It was as if time stopped, over and over. The intense moment was filled with the mystery of God coming to us, giving Christ's self for each one of us, and making us all one. Each pair of eyes reflected God's glory; God's presence was a living reality in the sharing of the sacrament.

The wondrous words of Christ will never sound the same again. "Take and eat; this is my body, given for you." ... "This cup is the new covenant in my blood, shed for you and for all people for the forgiveness of sin."

Remember, You are Dust
by Larry Morris

"Remember you are dust
And to dust you shall return".
Smeared and spoken.
Harsh
Jarring
Strange
Odd
Distant.

"Remember you are dust
And to dust you shall return".
My time is limited.
An end is coming.
I am not forever.

"Remember you are dust
And to dust you shall return".
Among all the possibilities
God deemed to create me.
To make me out of the chaos,
out of the dust,
then, to call me "child"
and claim me,
with promise, forever

"Remember you are dust
And to dust you shall return".
I am dust.
I am finite.
I am loved.
Endlessly.
Life as gift,
again.
Remember

Whispers From The Black Hole
by RuthAnn Wilson

Halfway through preparing my weekly Sunday School lesson, I cradled my head in my arms and sobbed, "God, how can I teach this to kids when I am not sure any of its true myself?" Scissors, paper and glue were ready, Bible passages marked, and the lesson book reviewed. But my heart plummeted once again into the dread fear that I was teaching a lie.

I asked Jesus into my heart when I was seven years old. I grew up faithfully reading my Bible, with plans to become a missionary doctor. I loved my church and family. I enjoyed school, especially reading; I loved exploring the woods near our farm with my dog and horse. I enjoyed learning new crafts and creating things, and cooking for the family when Mom had to work in the barn.

But shortly after my sixteenth birthday, my family moved to a new town and a new school. I was angry about leaving my friends and my school, and in my new school I got involved with things I believed were sin for me: smoking, some drinking. I didn't spend much time thinking about it, I just lived for the day, harboring my anger about having to move, and deciding I didn't care anymore. That was the beginning of a dreadful black hole in my heart, a sickness of the soul.

Soon after high school graduation, I put aside my plans for college and career. November came, and with it, my wedding day. Within a short time, I had three healthy, beautiful daughters. They were the center of my life, the joy of my heart. Holding them, reading to them, praying with them at meals and bedtime, I felt my life was nearly complete. I wanted them to know and love Jesus the way I had. I did everything I knew to have our family live a faithful, Christian life.

Nevertheless, that black hole sometimes whispered to me, "You're living a lie." My desire was to know Jesus more fully, follow Him more completely, and allow Him to be the center of my life. But the sins of my past tormented me. In my private devotions these verses leaped out at me:
> "*No one who puts his hand to the plow and looks back is fit for service in the kingdom of God."* (Luke 9:62)
> *"Be ye therefore perfect, even as your Father in heaven is perfect."* (Matthew 5:48)

I believed I had failed in following Christ faithfully during my late teens. I felt that what I had done was the equivalent of "hand to the plow and looking back," therefore, I was not fit for the kingdom of God. Furthermore, I understood it to mean I was without hope, because I knew no matter how hard I tried, I could not be perfect. These thoughts tormented me when I looked into my own heart.

On the outside, I looked like a good mother, a faithful Sunday School teacher, and a fine Christian. From the outside, I looked pretty good. But in the night, the whisper came again, "You are living a lie."

I cried out, "Lord God, prove yourself to me. I must know You are real, or I am just going to give up. Please show me someone who really and truly lives for You." Inside my head, I screamed, I begged, and I pleaded for God to prove Himself to me.

The black hole whispered in the background.

The next day, I asked my pastor if he had any books I could read that would help me. He opened his library to me, and I read some helpful books in the next few weeks.

Then it was time for our women's Bible study to meet again. A woman new to our area joined our group that day. As we were introduced, we discovered many shared interests. Several days later we met for coffee. During our conversation I could sense she truly knew and served God. Christ was first in her life, and the Bible was His living Word to her. He was indeed real to her. I felt uplifted and encouraged. I thanked God for using her to show me God was real.

For the next few days, I read my Bible every spare minute for many hours a day. I read with many questions, but also with renewed eagerness and hope. Late one April evening, I was home alone, reading in bed. The black hole whispered. My tears flowed and I begged God to show me what I needed to know.

Suddenly, it seemed as if passages of my Bible were shining under a radiant light and turning to just the passages I needed. Every word dazzled with God's grace and mercy for me. The whole room filled with the presence of Jesus. Indescribable joy filled me. I KNEW beyond a shadow of doubt God is real and God loves me just as I am! God's forgiveness and unconditional love is forever mine.

The black hole was healed; silenced forever and filled with God's Holy Spirit. With confidence in God's reality and presence, I finished preparing the lesson for Sunday.

2. Life and Love Stories

Me Do It
by RuthAnn Wilson

Once upon a time, there was a little girl whose first words were "Me do it."

If her mother reached down to tie her shoes, she backed away and said, "Me do it."

If she went with her parents to the orchard to pick apples, and if they spotted one big apple way high in the tree, she hollered, "Me do it!"

If her daddy took her for a walk in the woods, with reminders to stay in sight and not to cross the creek, the little girl whispered to herself, "Me do it."

Little Me-do-it's parents thought little girls should be quiet and obedient, not too independent.

They worried that she would get hurt.

Deep inside, Me-do-it was afraid she was disappointing her parents, but she just couldn't stop saying "me do it" no matter how hard she tried.

After many years, the little girl grew up and she grew old.

One night she bravely quavered, "Me do it", but she no longer had the strength.

She thought to herself, "I can't do it."

She looked up - and she let go.

"Please, help me."

"You do it."

And she closed her eyes.

My Father's Hat
by Beverly Berg

My father's hat hung on a nail that had cracked the thick cottonwood log. It hung above the wood box, next to the big black kitchen stove. That is – whenever he wasn't wearing it. And he wore it everywhere, even to the outhouse.

We all remembered the fantastic day that the new Western hat was being hung on the nail. Mom had won the first prize of fifty dollars when she entered a contest on safety driving. We couldn't believe it since she could only drive a team and wagon. She had bought chickens. But she said she had some money left.

We noticed that Dad was looking at a certain page in the Montgomery Ward Catalogue which contained western hats. Every time he picked up the catalogue, he'd just stare at a certain hat. We all knew how much he wanted that hat. The hat he wore was an old straw hat filled with holes which he had hung on that same nail.

Mom hadn't said anything to Dad, but had mailed an order for the hat several weeks ago when they had gone to town. She thought the hat might be in the post office now. It was my turn to go to the post office in town with Dad. We were all excited! Before we left from home, mom had told us to be sure and check in at the post office because she was expecting a package. Dad's face lit up. I think he guessed it was the hat.

It took a couple of hours for Sam and Shorty to pull our wagon into town. There was a place close to the train station for them. They stood under big cottonwood trees with other teams who had come to town and drank from a tub of water.

Dad and I stood on the railroad platform waiting and hoping that the black, noisy engine that pulled the train would bring the hat. When the train stopped, Jed Stravinski, the mailman, put a sack on a small cart. It bounced up and down as Jed pushed the cart down the dusty, bumpy main street on its way to the post office. I looked anxiously at the sack hoping to see a large lump. But the canvas was thick and smooth and there was no way to tell.

Dad and I followed behind and waved and shouted to the proprietors of the small stores we walked by on that street. The druggist, who had seen the small procession, came out of his store and handed Dad a small package. "Better not let yourself get so low on nitro, Everett. How many times do I have to tell you? You can't run out of those pills when you have angina! I'll give you a larger dose come winter in case you get house bound." Dad looked down. "Don't worry. You can pay me when you can."

The tavern stood next door to the drug store and Dad hesitated because I knew he could smell the beer. He didn't have any money but he had lots of friends. I pulled on his hand because if he went in, he might forget to come out and miss all the excitement of the hat. I was pretty sure he knew. We paused at the bank because I wanted to see if the boards had been removed from the door. But they were still there. Dad had told me that the whole country had run out of money and that he would have to borrow some money from the government. He could do this because he had served in the war and the government still hadn't completely paid their salary.

The small parade stopped now in front of Jed's post office. The post office looked small and insignificant where it stood beside the large bank. But Jed didn't think it was insignificant. He thought his post office was remarkably important. Jed picked up the mail bag and kicked open the door. He went through another door that was behind the mail boxes. "There must be about one hundred mail boxes," I said to Dad. I took our key from Dad and opened our box, but there was no mail. I was getting impatient. It seemed to take Jed a long time to open that sack and see if there was a package for us. But when I saw him come to the small post office window with a box in his hands, I knew it was the hat. The look on Dad's face told me that he knew it too. "Well, it come, by George. I figured it would come on the 4:10. We'd better wait until we get back to the wagon and not open it in the post office," Dad said. "It's a long way home and we'll have plenty of time to open it there." But I knew he was just as anxious as I was.

As I sat next to Dad on the way home I wondered if a king could have been as happy wearing a gold crown as Dad was wearing his brand new hat. "Dang fine hat! Best western hat in the catalogue!" he said. His deep blue eyes had twinkled with delight as he made a deeper crease down its middle. He slapped Sam and Shorty's rumps with the rein to move them ahead a little faster. I knew he was anxious to get home so he could show off the hat.

When we opened the kitchen door, there stood my two sisters, my brother and Mom, all with the happiest looking faces I had ever seen. Dad snatched the old straw hat from the nail and replaced it with his new one. He took the straw hat and stood in front of the cook stove. He took the tool and opened up the griddle. The fire was burning brightly as he dropped the hat into the flames.

Thank You Robinson Crusoe
by Beverly Berg

The prison in Illinois where I worked as a reading specialist was built in a farming area, and in the Fall was circled by beautiful green corn standing at least eight feet high which could be seen through the tall wire fence encircling the prison.

Smoke rose into the sky from chimneys in a small rural town about a mile away.

The classes ran from first grade up through two years of college. Trades were also taught by teachers from a neighboring college. They taught auto works, furniture refinishing, and cooking.

Most of my students were from the inner city of Chicago. Many of them had lived with their grandmothers because often one or the other of the parents were in prison, or on drugs. Some of the kids used to say, "I wish I'd listened to my grand-ma-ma. She used to walk me to the front door of the school, and I'd go out the back door to the gang."

I worked hard with phonics because the African American kids didn't use some of the English sounds in their speech; for example, the "g" in "ing". They'd say "comin," "goin."

One day the warden asked me if I'd attempt to teach an older man (about my age) who had never learned to read. When he was around twelve, a white man had called his father a "dirty nigger", punched him out, and threw him in the ditch. The kid went home, got his father's gun and shot the white man.

"He's been in and out of prison all of his life," the warden said; "and understandably hates 'whitey'".

The next morning, there was a knock on my classroom door. A guard had brought the new student (who was quite handsome) standing about six feet tall with beautiful teeth.

He looked down as he said to me, "The warden said you could teach me to read, but I don't think so."

He turned and started to leave, but I grabbed him by the arm, started to pull him into the classroom, and said, "Oh, I think you can!" The guard's mouth dropped open, as it is against the rules to touch a prisoner.

"Don't write me up," I said to him.

"I think the warden will understand." He smiled, nodded and left.

"His name is Robert, Teach," the other students said to me.

"Well, Robert," I said. "I think you came on a good day. I always begin the class by reading to the guys, and today I'm just starting a new book, called Robinson Crusoe. I'll tell you a little bit about what the story is about.

Robinson Crusoe tells how a terrible storm drowned all of his shipmates and left him marooned on a deserted island. Forced to overcome despair, doubt, and self-pity, he struggles to create a life for himself in the wilderness. Later in the story, he rescues a man from cannibals who he named Friday, and the man becomes his trusted companion."

The students always begged me to read a little more when I finished for the day. This was a new experience for them because often their parents were unable to read, and they were never read to.

Robert still wasn't looking at me, but was forced to look at the chalk board when I began the phonics. I started with the sounds from the letters of the words, "The man is mad at me." It was important that Robert have success right away. The other students knew what I was doing.

At the end of the first week, Robert could read and write, "The man is mad at me." plus a long list of words I had given him to memorize. The students all clapped for him. And Robert jumped up and down yelling, "I can read! I can read!"

Time went on with Robert making great progress. He was looking at me now, and laughing with me, along with the other students. But Robinson Crusoe was always the best part of the day; and when Friday arrived in the book, Robert was so excited, he said, "Teach! Teach! He has a friend! He has a friend" It was interesting to see grown men so excited about a book.

The time came rather quickly when Robert was able to read at a fourth grade level and was then able to learn the trade of his choice. He wanted to learn both cooking and furniture refinishing.

Some of the new students coming into the classroom appeared "turned off" and were not cooperating. So, one day I went over to Robert's classroom where he was learning furniture refinishing.

I asked his teacher if I could speak with him because I had the feeling that he would be able to help the new students gain enough confidence so that they'd be able to start learning to read.

The next day, there was a knock on the door, and when I opened it, in walked Robert wearing a confident smile. He picked up a reader from my desk, opened it to his favorite story, and began to read rather loudly with a great deal of confidence, the smile never leaving his face.

"Okay Group, see what I can do? And it didn't take me very long either. It was Fast! Fast! Fast!—and I couldn't read a word when I came in here. So, you guys better get down to work—right now—and start learning because I'll be back soon to check!" The students were very attentive and quiet. "O. K., we'll work," they said. And they did!

Robert had just about finished serving his sentence and was about to be released. The warden had located a cooking job for him, so I hoped he wouldn't be back. He had continued reading because I had seen him in the library checking out books.

The day he was to leave he had gotten permission from the warden to come into my classroom and say good-byes. It was a new Robert that entered the classroom that last day. He was wearing a wine-colored suit and was full of smiles.

"I came to say good-bye," he said, "and to thank you for teaching me to read." (I noticed he said "teaching" instead of "teachin". He shook my hand.

" I have something for you, Robert," I said as I pulled open a desk drawer and handed him <u>Robinson Crusoe.</u>

Valentine's Day
by Beverly Berg

The calendar that hung on a nail that was pounded into a log in our house had a picture on it of a big red heart. Yes! It was Valentine's Day.

My Dad was hitching up Sam and Shorty to the wagon for a trip to town, and I was going along. I grabbed the bag of eggs that I had packed in straw, and climbed into the wagon. I sat beside him and held the reins while he rolled and lit a cigarette. He lifted his chin as he blew the smoke into the small flakes of falling snow.

We traveled on a trail that wound through the badlands in sparsely settled North Dakota. We wanted to make it in time to meet the train. We both loved it. Sometimes my Dad worked in the engine shoveling coal into the fire that produced the steam that made the engine go.

We had about fifteen miles to go and made it in plenty of time to see the train come in. As we tied up the team behind the boarded up bank where they had food and water, we heard the whistle blow, and walked quickly to the depot. My Dad's face lit up with a smile as the big black engine roared in and stopped, making a hissing sound of steam. The coal car behind the engine was piled high with coal, and trailing behind were the railroad cars filled with the sounds of cattle. But – on top of these cars was a line of sitting men riding through the country looking for work. They knew this was a water-stop for the engine to take on water, which gave them time to jump down, and maybe find some food. The people in this small town were generous and shared what little they had with these hungry men.

I saw a very young man, who looked about seventeen, jump down. "Dad," I said, "could I talk to him?"

"I think it's a good idea, Bev, he looks hungry."

"Well, hello," I said, "my name is Beverly. What's yours?"

"I'm John," he said. "Thanks for talking to me. I just left my Grandparents to find work, but I am a little lonesome, so thanks for the hello." He looked at my Dad and asked, "Are there jobs around here?"

"No," my Dad answered, "but I think if you go on as far as Miles City, Montana, you might get lucky."

"Thanks," he said. "My Grandparents are running out of food."

"I have some eggs," I replied. "You look hungry. We can scramble them at my Mom's friend Betty's house just down the street. Our chickens did great this week!"

"I'll be right behind," Dad said. "I have to stop at the post office. Some of my Vet friends have received a long overdue check from the government for back pay from the War. It's been a long time coming, but maybe we'll get lucky, and I'll be able to pay the bill at the grocery store, and oh, Boy! Do I need some tobacco! Wish me luck!"

"I'll say a prayer," I answered, as John and I started down the street toward Betty's house. We could smell some homemade bread as we knocked on the door.

John smiled while he ate the high pile of eggs, and hot bread. Just then my Dad came in with the biggest smile I have ever seen on his face. "It come! By George, it come! I paid the grocery store, got tobacco, and still have some left." He handed John a five dollar bill. "I don't want you hungry until you get that job!"

John's eyes filled with tears. "Thank you, sir. I'll pay you back."

"Well, thanks, God," I said, "for answering my prayer."

"We'd better start back to the depot," I said. "It's almost time to get to Miles city."

Betty handed John an addressed, stamped envelope with paper and a pen inside.

Sometime later we did hear from John. He had found a job at a dairy, and said he was very busy learning to milk cows. He was invited to stay at the farm with the owners, and would receive a small check which he would send to his Grandparents.

Also in the envelope was a five dollar bill for my Dad. At the end of the letter he wrote, "Thank you for the greatest Valentine's Day of my life."

Those Tears
by Marlene Obie

Why did she not cry
when he passed from this life?
It was not that she no longer cared.
He'd been leaving for years
little chunks at a time.
She'd already shed those tears.

She'd mourned with him often
along the decades
as his quality of life wore thin.
Expectations and plans lay
smushed in the guck of the mud
from the rain of her tears.

She knew well the demons,
the pain they inflicted.
She'd tried to help chase them away.
But she had to pull back
and save her own soul
lest she drown in a bloodbath of tears.

While sharing their lives for 47 years,
they'd learned where they fit and what didn't.
Over mountains, in valleys,
on beaches, through deserts,
they'd shaken out laughter and tears.

Over life's edge, beyond all his fears,
he has gone with relief, she believes.
She may breathe out a sigh,
but her eyes remain dry,
for she already cried those tears.

Fields of Earth, Field of Love
by Pastor Larry Morris

The ground, the earth, dirt, acreage, the fields - are its names.

My home sits on it. Our roads lay across it.
It is one of life's dimensions

For a century my family has planted in it, and harvested on it.
It has provided them with sustenance and life.

Labor has been given to it
and its fruits have been received with relief and thanks.

From it - corn and soybeans, hay and alfalfa, apples and pears, beans and tomatoes, watermelons and cantaloupe, cherries and peas have been grown and eaten and sold and enjoyed.

Beauty is seen in the growth on its acres. The tassels of corn and leaves of soybeans sway in the wind and tickle the heart.

Some of its produce is given only for joy; Marigolds, petunias, tulips, impatiens, gladiolas, geraniums and lobelia to name a few.

Now it is home for my father.
It is a blanket to hold him safe, till we all live as joy forever
in God's field of love.

3. Wisdom in Words

Shoreline
by Pat Mason

At the shoreline,
the tides ebb and flow.

As they have done
since time began.

Gradually they wear away,
what had once seemed so strong.

The sunrise and the sunset
in the high desert
also ebb and flow.
like the oceans' tides
at the faraway shore.

But in the high desert,
the wind is the current.

And the sky, not the deep,
is the great unknown.

Yet, as it is with the sailor,
so it is with the desert people,
and so it is throughout the world.

The truth for us all is the same.

The greatest hardships,
the greatest mysteries,
the greatest joys,
and the greatest sorrows,

all lie within the depths of our own unsettled souls.

February
    by Pat Mason

The light is increasing yet remains elusive.

The cold is decreasing yet still rules the days.

Springtime is promised but seems so far away.

Together we keep to ourselves, and we wait.

Even grim winter days are not to be wasted.

Such moments as these shall not come again.

So let us keep still, as the season dictates.

As the heart continues to beat and grow,

And ache and love;

Held graciously in the hand of God.

Creatrix
by Ruth Hanley

I have carried a piece of you since my beginning
you are a part of me
waiting inside for your dance with life
you are a piece of my heart
what hurts you hurts me
what pleases you pleases me
one day
the doctors sliced me open and lifted you out
                              away
now you are a bird wandering too far from your nest
the invisible cord that anchors you to me is stretched
too tight
snap
now you can fly

Little Ivy Thoughts
by Marlene Obie

They enter softly and slowly, creeping under, through and over surfaces that have seen better years and desperately need some restyling.

They flaunt deceptive, decorative appeal of unique shapes and interesting splotches of sheen and fool us into believing we're favored by their presence.

When our attention turns for just a blink, their roots bore deep and outward, silently speed-weaving an entrenched net with which to trap and control.

One day we awake and notice our entire yard has been invaded and ivy has sprawled like a tightly woven carpet over everything in its path.

While we clip and pull at these invasive intruders, they sink lower and wait for our distraction toward the more conspicuous.

Then up they pop up and taunt our attempts to feel good about our open, untangled growth.

Help us Master Gardener to find every last hidden thread and dig it out that we might flourish freely.

Thankful for Living
    by Suzanne Morris

To smell a forest
    After the rain

To see the sun
    Breaking through the clouds

A dawning of the world
    Clean and bright

So fresh
    As the first day of creation

To see colors shining
    Through the grayness before

Looking at all the forms
    Of all the things God created

Wondering at
    The birds on wing
        Or the rabbit scurrying through the underbrush

All the sounds
    You begin to hear

A chirp
    A rustle
        The breeze blowing through the trees

You stand in the midst of it all
    A small part of the whole

And you feel thankful for living

Self! Shut Up Your Murmuring!
by Marlene Obie

I complain about
the cold weather outside
while I sit on my bed
in my cozy fleece robe,
amid comfort-filled quilts
from family and friends.
Here in my own room full of books,
mementoes, partially finished projects,
a closet crammed with clothing,
some just taking up space,
and "my life and loved ones"
picture gallery, I sip hot tea,
play games and communicate electronically.

In open exposure and barest
of shelters, some hunker down
under whatever scrounged materials
might offer protection from elements
of weather, disasters, or
human acts of violence.
Vital and sentimental possessions;
loved ones as well, lost or
abandoned in haste for survival.
With growling stomachs
they doze and pray
for a little relief.

Self, just shut up your murmuring.
You should be ashamed.
And I am!

Never Walk Alone.
by Otto Brask

Sometimes you find the hand of God at work in places, where you least expect it. Maybe that is part of the great mystery of His relationship with us.

On a Saturday some time ago I turned on the TV in hope of watching the twelve o'clock news reports. Instead, an old episode of a Bill Cosby Show came on the tube. Having enjoyed Bill Cosby many times earlier, - his funny expressions and his comical remarks in awkward situations, - I relaxed and watched this rerun.
Dr. Huxtable, played by Bill Cosby, and his wife, Claire, visited their Alma Mater, Hillman College, where he was asked to be the M.C. at the graduation ceremony. After loosening up the faculty and the student body with his usual flair and self-inflicting, sarcastic remarks about his own college days, he introduced the main speaker, the retiring College President.
The white haired, aging, black professor, in his departing speech to the graduating class, - to the best of my recollection - said the following:
"I'll tell you, what I'm not gonna speak about. I will not talk about social justice and equality. You all know my thoughts on those topics. I will not talk about racial issues and I will not talk about peace on earth, because you all know, where I stand in regards to these matters. I will address something, which concerns me about your future:

When, - 20 years from now, when you are twice your age today and a success in whatever field you choose to devote your life to, - you receive a phone call from a Hillman College student asking for your advice because of your wisdom and knowledge on important matters, - get in your car, drive one or two hundred miles and pick up that student, - invite him or her

out for a sumptuous dinner and lavish upon this person some of your experience, your insight in public affairs and your love for your fellow human beings,- <u>for he or she should never walk alone!</u> " (End of speech)
I did not expect this provoking message from a lighthearted comedy show. This was not just a nice speech of good wishes to the students at graduation. This brief statement challenges all of us in our relationship to each other. Yes, it is a call to action in our daily lives. <u>- For he or she should never walk alone! –</u>
You may not be called upon to travel 100 miles to advise or console a student from your alma mater. And I pray you shall not have to respond to an early morning phone call from your vagrant son or daughter in a hospital 1000 miles away, following a midnight car accident
But you might assist a neighbor, who needs a hand babysitting or help her with transportation to the doctor. You might visit a lonesome, aging person with Alzheimer's or take time to console a grieving friend, who needs a shoulder to lean on.

Let not the opportunity to render assistance slip away, - <u>for he or she should never walk alone!</u>

By the grace of God, may we be found worthy and willing to help and comfort our fellow human beings in need.

We too shall never walk alone, for this is the promise of Jesus, His departing words of the Gospel of Matthew: "And remember, I will be with you always to the end of time ".

Three Baby Banty Chicks
by RuthAnn Wilson

Early one May morning, when the leaves on the willows were nearly the size of a mouse's ear, Mother Hen stood up and stretched her wings. There were 3 eggs remaining in her nest. Near the large gray boulder in the meadow, Mother Hen had been working hard. For many days, she had been keeping all the eggs warm.

Each day and each night she had kept the eggs dry and warm under her wings. Now Mother Hen had nine yellow, fluffy, cheeping chicks gathered near. She waited patiently for her last three eggs to hatch.

The nine chicks were eager to try their legs and to begin searching for insects and for seeds to eat. Finally they could wait no longer. Mother Hen and the nine chicks began to peck and cheep their way across the meadow.

The three eggs in the nest were still warm. They were gently rocking, and tiny sounds could be heard from inside each egg. Small cracks appeared on the shell of one egg. Another egg had several holes in the shell. Something wet and yellow was wiggling inside. The third egg was beginning to open, and a tiny yellow beak was trying to push out of the egg.

Just then, a young girl came skipping across the meadow. She was happy to be out in the spring sunshine. She was on her way to the banks of the creek to pick yellow buttercups for her mother before breakfast.

But what was that? She stopped and listened. She heard the cheeping and chirping sounds of baby chicks. Then she saw Mother Hen and the nine chicks scattering across the meadow in search of food.

She looked down and saw the nest with the three eggs. She carefully kneeled down and looked closely. Gently, she reached out her finger and touched one of the eggs. It was warm. It felt like it was moving. She picked up the egg and held it lightly in the palm of her hand.

The cracks on the shell were opening. She could see the beak of the baby chick pushing on the egg shell. The little girl wondered if the baby chick needed help to get the shell off. Very gently, she picked at a piece of loose shell. She lifted it off. The baby chick's beak moved again. It was trying to get out of the eggshell. The little girl carefully removed another piece of eggshell. Very, very slowly, and very, very carefully, the little girl tried to help the baby chick get out of the shell.

Finally, the shell was off. The baby chick tried to lift its head. It tried again. Then the baby chick rested for a few moments. Soon it moved its beak and tried to get up. It rested again. Then it stopped moving. The little girl was afraid. Why wasn't the little chick getting up?

The little girl looked at the other two eggs. One of the eggs was empty! Then she heard a baby chick behind her. Just as she turned around, that baby chick saw Mother Hen and ran over to her.

Then the little girl looked at the last egg. It was lying quietly in the nest. The little girl picked it up. It was cold now, and nothing moved. Then the little girl looked down at the little chick she had helped out of the nest. That chick was not moving. It felt cold.

Suddenly the little girl felt cold all over. She wondered what was wrong. Why was the egg so cold now? Why was the little chick cold now? Why was everything so quiet now? The little girl felt very sad. She wanted to know what had happened. She wished she could ask somebody. She had been trying so hard to help the baby chicks, and now something was wrong. The baby chick that she tried to help was so cold. Was it dead? Why was the other egg just lying there?

But the baby chick that she did not help was gone with its mother. It was strong and healthy, and running merrily across the meadow with its brothers and sisters. It was chirping happily as it ran to find another tasty seed to eat.

Several years later the little girl learned that baby chicks need to struggle on their own to get out of the shell in order to develop their strength to live. She learned that one should not help someone to do what one should do for oneself.

Water
by Pat Mason

Water is not what it appears to be when Jesus speaks of it.
Fortified cities take on a new meaning.
Circumcision as a word can symbolize a state of heart.
Breath means more than a physical movement of air.
Birth is not just a human act.
Veils, vision and healing cannot be taken at face value.
Gates, neighbors and things possible need to be redefined.
If all these and more are changed with God,
what then of our understanding of life and death?

Listening to the Thunder
by Kim Deskin

I live in a part of the country, now,
  where thunderstorms are rare.
I grew up, however, where
  lightening, thunder, and rain
  were daily activity.

Tonight, the lightning flashes
  out my window.
I count one one thousand
    two one thousand
  up to twelve, and I know
  it will be twelve minutes
  before the rain is pouring.

A few minutes pass.
I finish some work on the computer,
  actually relishing in the quiet
    of the house. It's so rare.

Lightning flashes.
Five one thousands pass.
I contemplate the Zeus angle. He
  sending warnings to Earth.
Demanding obedience. Demanding concern.

I hope my children won't be awakened
  and frightened, as I was ages ago.

Memories draw me into writing,
    as the raindrops start to fall.

Now the lightening and the thunder
    almost match.

The rain falls harder.
We've had more thunder in this
    part of the country in the last few
    months. Are the gods trying to
    tell us something? Are we awry?
    Are we too warming the globe?
    or simply not attending the need.

Oddly, the rain on the roof
    and the lightening in the sky
    and the thunder accompanying all,
(despite my internal controversy)
are almost comforting.
    Maybe it's the writing.

The rain lessens.
  A flash catches my eye.
    We're back to five one thousands,
    but the thunder is still deep.
    My Zeus won't let me leave him.
    He wants to make an impression.
        To tell me to be calmed in the chaos.
        To know that the storm will abate.

Funny, as I run out of words, the storm
has moved itself back to twelve minutes away.
The raindrops dwindle. The children sleep.
And I marvel that such a soft storm
        could have such a strong impact.

Time Trials
by Marlene Obie

Time drags, that's a gift.
    Jump on, take a ride, nap, just be?

There's time enough, or is that an illusion?
    What is the measure of its line in the sands of time?

Running a race with changing times,
    getting ahead of them, falling behind.

Time on my hands with time to spare;
    take time now, or make it up on the way.

Where's the department of lost and found time?
    Is a time manager in the nick of it?

Time is money; it counts.
    When is borrowed time due? Is it yet? Or now?

Will time tell how many stitches are in a time saver?
    Is that info time sensitive?

Time flies. Can I catch them up to hold in a bottle?
    Would I be a time killer and have to serve it?

Time waits for no one; it marches on.
    Am I stepping in it as it passes?

Does biding my time in its crunches
    extend the prime time of my life?

Do all things keep time for every matter?
    At all times, every, any or some?

When timing is off, short, tight, or tough,
    can I trust time to heal all wounds or will it run out?

I think due time is ripe now for picking and sharing
    sweet fruits from the fullness of time.

The test of time ticks off my moments in time,
    which in their essence clearly appear
    to be up for the time of my life.

Attitude
by Marlene Obie

Attitude is everything.
It's the magic crayon
I create my world with.
I can pick it up and color away
or drown in a vapor of gray.

Yes, it's scary to place a mark
of purple on my pages
and live with intention
I might create an existence
that provokes my spirit to smile,
changes my perspectives
and inspires me to draw modified
or completely new adventures.

What kind of silly drawing might
emerge from doodling along.
with no particular agenda or
goals for a while? Just imagine
the fun of chasing rainbows
and mixing up their auras
with large splats of nonsense!
If I get into the wild, crazy whirl of it,
Who knows what I might be?

The choices of shades and hues
for dabbling in boggle my mind
so much that I'm kind of inclined
to retreat to my critical ink scratches,
my blinding white expectations,
my safe, gray anesthesia.

No, I think not!

I'll take up that yellow one,
draw some daffodils onto the snow,
and grab neon-bright tints of
humor, faith and hope
to splatter into my outlook.

A little here, a little there.
There now, attitude,
Now, you're looking good!

The Preacher's Ballet Slippers
By Pastor Larry Morris

Once upon a time
there was a little girl
who couldn't sit still for very long.
After a short time sitting
she would simply have to stand
and then move and then dance
and then smile.

Her parents were scared
to take her to church
where people sit
for a long time.
At the first church they visited,
people glared when she moved
so she sadly sat on her hands
and thought of other things.

At the next church,
after seven loooooong minutes,
she began to slowly move
to the beat of the hymn
the congregation was singing.
A grandmother sitting across the aisle smiled.

During the offering
the little girl danced in the aisle
and smiled inside and out.
When she opened her eyes
everyone around her was smiling at her joy.

When her parents opened their eyes
their fear went away.

Today that little girl is all grown up.
and she is the pastor of that church
and she preaches in ballet slippers.

Negativity
by Marlene Obie

Negativity kills.
Like a worm, it works its way into
our bodies and souls, festers and
spreads its infection across our spirits,
battering our complacent cells into
fields of stubble where weeds of
depression, anxiety, anger, and
hopelessness sprout, and smother
seeds of creativity and joy.

I will not, cannot let it latch onto me.
No matter that greed, cruelty and stupidity abound.
No matter that hard times throw out nets.
of confusion and doubt.
No matter that despair spreads tentacles
throughout my brain intending to suck me in.

It doesn't matter, doesn't matter,
for I am a child of God, born
of feminine and masculine image with
eyes to see beauty in the meanest environment,
ears to hear soul symphonies amid a clanging,
squawking cacophony of anger and criticism.

Though a thick mist of gloom assails me,
it will not block out my faith in sunshine.
I call upon the Spirit of the Living God
which frees me from negativity's net and
restores heart-blood of compassion,
goodness, love and mercy
into my veins, attitude and commitment.

For I am a Child of God!

4. Just for Fun

The Problem with Easter
by Ruth Hanley

Honey, the Easter Bunny is coming to our house!
Yes, just like Santa did but for a different reason
Though I don't exactly know why.
He leaves eggs
no, I don't know where he gets them
Or why he leaves them
And none of them will be in your basket
Just two stuffed animals
Chocolate (some of that is for me, honey)
Some books
Candy
And your Easter outfit.
Didn't I tell you?
We'll wear new clothes to church on Easter Sunday
To symbolize new life
Um…is that correct?
Jesus died…well, I'll explain 'die' later
like Grandma did
And then he rose again
That means that people got to see him
For a little bit
No, Grandma didn't do that part
And then he went to heaven
Just like Grandma
But sort of in a more important way
Because he was God's son
And that is why the Easter Bunny is coming to our house
Just like the one we saw at the mall!
Because he loves you
Just like we do.

The Effect of Alcohol
by Minna Brask

It was my father's birthday. I had saved a little money and bought one bottle of lager beer. I wrapped it nicely, and presented it to him in the morning. It was a holiday so he was home that day. Thus he enjoyed the beer with his lunch.

After the meal we watched my younger brother (probably three or four years old) reach for the bottle, which had a little left at the bottom. Reverently he lifted it to his mouth while my father watched him with a smug grin, probably thinking that the little guy would cough and spit it onto the floor, however, my brother just deferentially lowered the bottle and exclaimed:

""Ahhh - good stuff!"

A Ghost Story
by Minna Brask

After a year of living in an apartment in Seattle, my husband and I found and bought a little house in the outskirts of Kirkland and Bothell with a Woodinville address. We moved in on our first wedding anniversary, borrowing a friend's pickup truck to move our few belongings. Friends of ours lent a set of beds, and we managed with a picnic table along with a small table and three old chairs for furniture. We made due with that until my furniture from Denmark arrived.

The house was the last of four houses on a dirt road, which ended at our property. It was a heavily wooded area with second growth trees. A few of the old stumps stood as a reminder of a time, when pioneers explored and harvested the old growth with hand saws and transported the timber to the saw mills on horse drawn wagons.

There was much to do in and around the little house, making it ready for my father's arrival the spring thereafter. We had little time to explore the back area of our two-acre property, but one day we took an ax and a saw with us, and made our way to the back. It was very dense woods, which nobody had penetrated for years. Therefore, at the very back we were surprised to find a complete skeleton of a horse.

Somebody had probably ended its life of misery and left it there.

When our friends brought their children over for visits, we took them to see the skeletal remains. At Halloween time especially, the children enjoyed the thrill of the ghostly reminders. For a while they stood quietly in awe and reverence, so I felt I had to break the spell.

You should have seen their faces, when I in a gloomy voice added:

"But we never found the rider!"

Big Old House on the Corner
by Pastor Larry Morris

It was a big old white house on the corner
with three bedrooms
and one bathroom
and it housed seven of us.

We ate in the kitchen,
did our homework in the living room,
jumped on the beds,
sang into the window fans,
threw toy parachute army men
out the upstairs windows,
practiced tennis against the garage door,
put up storm windows in the winter,
and screens in the summer,
played ping pong on the porch,
played catch in the yard,
and flew kites in the neighborhood.

We ate and learned to cook eggs and pancakes,
roast beef and fried chicken,
green beans and creamed corn,
hamburger and tuna casserole,
spaghetti and soup,
oyster stew and kumla,
lefse and potato cakes,
chocolate chip cookies and pudding.
fudge and popcorn!

We broke a collar bone and arm,
burnt a hand on the oven,
nearly burned that house down,
entertained aunts and uncles
grandparents and cousins
and sat on the same sofa for 25 years,

We poured a new driveway and sidewalk,
put up paneling and new ceilings
painted the walls over and over
mowed the lawn
vacuumed the carpets and
washed a million dishes
all by hand

Then we all grew up
and moved away
to new places
to make new memories
in new homes
with our new families.
But there's nothing like the
home you grew up in.

Thanks Mom and Dad.
Thanks sisters and brothers.
And thanks big old white house on the corner.

5. On Friendship and Family

On My Way to the Sudoku
by David Patneaude

On my way to the Sudoku I glance at the obituary page and glimpse a familiar smile on a familiar face and my breath abandons me, leaving an aching vacuum in my chest, because I saw this familiar man—James, the obituary says, but I knew him as someone with the more affable name Jim—only a couple of weeks ago, full of life, in the locker room at the Y, where we traded pleasantries almost daily, and he gave me his usual hello then, as always a little wistful but amiable in a genuine sort of way.

He had arthritis, an affliction that slowed his walk and stooped his shoulders, but didn't keep him from greeting the guys dressing nearby or wandering past, and everyone said hi back at him, which is how I came to know his name (formal introductions don't fly when you're half-naked or dripping sweat).

He was a lap swimmer, and I once asked him about his swim fins and he took the time to tell me about them and where to find them and how much they cost. I never bought any—I'm a dry land kind of exerciser—but you never know.

The fins propelled us into a chance to talk, something beyond a nod and a grunt.

The bare-bones obituary says he was 63—an age that I once thought was old, but not now. It says he had a dad and some cousins. That's it. It doesn't mention the men at the Y who enjoyed seeing his smile and exchanging a few friendly words with him and now wish they'd done more.

It doesn't say how he died. It doesn't say how empty the locker room seems these days.

If a guy dies at 63, he shouldn't be written off, he should be written about, his obituary should say more, especially if he's someone whose smiling photo can catch my eye— and pilfer my breath—on my way to the Sudoku.

Co-Sleeper's Neck
by Ruth Hanley

Rhythmic breathing and lazy suck of the pacifier
tells me that it's time to remove my body from the
foot
of her bed.
I slowly get up
and replace myself with a cheap princess replica
my feet avoid the electronic devices in the room
designed to set off alarms in singsong voices
to let her know I am leaving the room.
practiced hands open the door without the squeak
I creep back into the bed at 2am and find my husband's feet
to let him know that all is well.
Over the monitor, I hear the anticipated deep sigh
A signal that I am granted another few hours of sleep.

Gourmand
by Ruth Hanley

"mmm it's sweet" says Mom
lifting a spear of asparagus
out of the can
curved
and dripping

graham crackers in milk
are good at first bite
mushy paste at the next
and the next

sandwiches made with liver
squeezed from a tube
taste like a sick cheese

"so good"
says Mom
she takes a bite
and sees a familiar old kitchen table
5 girls
and two parents
knit together by strong yarns
laughter
and comfort food.

"Berries? Go Berries?"
by RuthAnn Wilson

"Berries? Go berries?" I loved to go berry-picking with my Mom, to hear the chinkling of juicy blackberries piling up in the pail, and later to taste the warm burst of pleasure from Mom's pies.

Mom tied my sunbonnet under my chin, hung several nested pails on one arm and bundled my baby sister on her other arm. We trudged up the lane toward the East Forty, where the berries hung blackly from bushes, begging to be picked.

"Pail? Me pail?" I begged insistently, wanting to carry my own little pail.

After Mom carefully arranged newborn baby Mary on the blankets in a shady spot, she wiped the sweat from her brow as she handed me my little pail. "Here's your pail, honey. Now you stay right by me and don't get lost," she warned. I eagerly agreed; I wanted to be safe.

As Mom's pail began to rattle with warm, sweet fruit, the purple stain on my lips gave evidence that I, too, was picking blackberries. My little arms could not reach far, so I soon was around the corner of a blackberry bush where Mom couldn't see me. She was concentrating on filling her pail with berries so she could get back to the house and bake a pie for supper.

I placed several berries in my pail, walked a little farther, and ate the big ones I found there. I spied some even bigger ones a little farther on. When I got there, I found I couldn't reach them. Flies and bees were buzzing all around, and the sun seemed even hotter. I stooped to look at a bumble bee on a dandelion, and then picked the dandelion so I could blow the fuzz.

Soon I continued onward the search for more berries forgotten. I stumbled over a semi-dried cow pie on the cow path, and then sat down by it, entranced by the interesting way the flies were coming in and out. I poked at the cow pie; how interesting that it was hard on top but juicy underneath. Some of the juice squirted on my hands.

Birds cawing and calling caught my attention. I looked up. A bluebird was sitting right over there where I might catch it. Leaving the pail, I ran toward the bird, but it flew away. I tried to follow, but soon I couldn't see it any more. I began to cry.

Crying, scratching at bites on my arms and legs, and not seeing my Mom, I stumbled farther and farther toward the woods.

"Mommy! Mommy!" I cried and cried.

I was at the edge of a creek, with water swirling in eddies around the rocks. Willows grew along the edge where the cows came to drink. I could go no farther, so I sat down, crying hard by now. I couldn't see anybody, and I heard scary sounds in the woods.

Sobbing, my panties wet with fear, I knew I was lost. No one was there. I was all alone. Some of my scratches were bleeding, and I had cow pie juice smeared all over. Verging on hysteria, I threw myself on the muddy bank of the creek and screamed.

Then I heard sounds of branches breaking and something running. Stopping my screams, I looked up, and flying across the river was my Daddy, his terror-filled face aimed straight for me. He scooped me into his arms as his tears joined with mine.

"Oh, Baby, Baby. My Tootsie, you're alright. It's going to be alright. I've got you now."

His arms tight around me, he carried me through the bushes and down the cow path toward home. I knew I was safe and secure in my Daddy's arms.

Song To My Friend
by RuthAnn Wilson

Friend, I'm grateful for the days we share,
Together sharing laughter, joy and fears,
Together lifting voices up in prayer;
Singing hopeful songs that wash away our tears.
Thank you, Friend, for listening to my dreams,
For helping me to sift the right from wrong,
For talking with me in the starlight gleams,
For seeking for the faith which makes us strong.

Our friendship grows from listening with our heart,
Through sharing stories of our girlhood days,
And searching out best ways to a new start.
O! Our love of beauty, earth, and children's play.
I'm thankful for our friendship fine and rare,
My friend, I'm glad that we can love and care.

Thirty Two Tiny Valentines
by Pastor Larry Morris

They still sell boxes of 32 tiny valentines
to school kids for $2.49,
so I bought one.
I wrote sweet nothings on them to my wife, my love.
When she fell asleep on the 13th
I put one next to her pillow.
Then the fun began.
One in her sock drawer,
another inside a favorite folded up sweater
and a couple inside shoes.
One in the left pocket of her house coat,
she uses that pocket less than the right pocket.
One in the pocket of a pair of slacks
and one that she won't find until June
put into the pocket of an old pair of shorts!

In the medicine cabinet
in the bathroom plant
the microwave
the silverware drawer
the refrigerator
the dry laundry detergent
buried in the freezer
and behind a can of diced tomatoes.

One inside a rarely used bowl
that I will have to work around
until she finds it.

One in the trunk of her car
and another in the glove compartment
which she may not find till… who knows when.

One in the book she's reading
a couple in her purse
and more in the pockets of her coats

One - I can't tell you where it is
(it would ruin the surprise)
and eight I have forgotten where they are.

Thirty two times I will tell her I love her
(for $2.49).

In the Midst of Darkness
by Pastor Larry Morris

When the ceiling above you is falling down..
and you feel the darkness closing in,
when the sadness is overwhelming
and you feel all alone,
a candle burns
and I will hold hope for you

When you don't have the energy to go on
and your dreams have gone up in smoke,
when all others have gone away
and depression fills your day,
a candle burns
and I will hold hope for you

I will hold your hand and not demand
I will hear your pain and cry beside
I will be near and see you, again and again
I will be near and see you again

When life goes blank and you are empty
and you fear your tears have no end,
when life seems to have no meaning
and your life seems worthless,
a candle burns
and I will hold hope for you

I will hold your hand and not demand
I will hear your pain and cry beside
I will be near and see you, again and again
I will be near and see you again

I will wait, for you are my friend
I will pray, for I am your friend

I will see you, for you are a part of me
and I will hold hope for you

I will hold your hand and not demand
I will hear your pain and cry beside
I will be near and see you, again and again
I will be near and see you again

6. Short Stories and a Sermon

The Family Auction
by Patricia Anderson

No one would have guessed my cousin Bob could auctioneer like a pro. Eighty of my family members, all descendants of Andrew and Carrie Anderson, sat in the cleaned barn with the smell of straw filling the air; how surprised they would be at this living legacy gathered in rural Minnesota! From across the country we had gathered, some of us meeting for the first time. The first event for the weekend of festivities was an auction where memorabilia from the Anderson family would be auctioned to the next generation. Cats walked among us with tails high, letting us know they were the kings and queens of the barn. Barn Swallows swooped to their nests confused by the two-legged creatures invading their living quarters. The horses were moved outside and blocked from their refuge. In the southwest corner of the barn posters with pictures of extended family groups were displayed. The center area held folding chairs in straight lines like empty church pews during the week. Soon, like church pews on a Sunday morning, the chairs would be filled.

This was the first "real" auction I had been to. The kind where I had to be careful; scratching my nose might be seen as a bidding signal. I remembered watching a movie where someone had purchased an extremely expensive item because they waved at a friend at the other side of the room. The thought was delightfully stressful; I smiled at the thought, then made a mental note to be careful when moving my hands!

Prior to any auction, there is a time for people in attendance to view the items to be sold. Many of us were milling around looking at the family items and reminiscing about what they remembered and where great grandma had placed this or that.

It was then that the item I wanted to buy, caught my eye. I had to have it! I had never seen anything like it. It wasn't old, but it was a treasure. It was a black and white afghan that somehow had the 1939 family picture of my great grandparents and their seven children woven into it! Having seen this picture many times at my grandparents' house, I was amazed to see it displayed on the afghan. How was this photograph transposed? Some new computer miracle I suppose. The result –a cold black and white photo became soft, warm and alive. How wonderful to be wrapped with such an afghan. It would be a group hug!

The auction began promptly at 2 pm. The first item up for bid was my great grandmother's wedding dress. It was not the usual white, but a beautiful robin's egg blue with puffed sleeves and rows of handmade lace. A cousin modeled the dress and the bidding began. " Fifty, fifty who'll give me fifty, sixty, who'll give me sixty?" The spotter never missed a hand or a nod and the bidding kept going up until I heard the words, sold for $250! I waited patiently for other items to be sold, Grandpa's shaving brush, Grandma's apron, a Bible, their Marriage License, a Confirmation Certificate, Grandpa's wallet (including driver's license), war ration coupons. Only two more to go, a 50th wedding anniversary table cloth and a wagon wheel.

Finally it was time for the afghan I had been waiting for. The bidding started at twenty. My hand shot up. "Who'll give me thirty?" The spotter kept busy with his crisp "yup" acknowledgement of the bidders. Should I keep bidding? Did someone want the afghan more than I? No, I wanted it more than anyone else. I had a special purpose for the treasure so I wouldn't stop bidding. Finally I heard the words "sold for $85.00".

Bob the auctioneer said "It looks like this afghan is going to Seattle". I stood up and said "No, not Seattle, it's going to Grandma Berg." My grandmother was the oldest child in the picture on the afghan. At 99 and living in a nursing home, she is alert mentally; sadly, she was not strong enough to make the trip to the family reunion. I knew her heart was with us and I wanted to share a piece of the celebration with her. I could hardly wait to visit her and give her this precious gift. She could wrap herself with her family in the cozy afghan. It would be like getting tucked in bed as a child. She could once again be surrounded by her loved ones of long ago. I realized at that moment, there's nothing like the love of a family, no matter how old you are.

Christmas Eve Sermon
by Pastor Katy McCallum Sachse

A mother crept into her young son's room during a loud and violent thunderstorm, for she had heard him crying. "What's the matter?" she asked. "I'm scared," said the boy. The mother began to talk to him about thunderstorms; that they were certainly loud and scary, but far away, and could not really hurt him. "I'm still scared," said the boy. The mother told him that she and his father were just downstairs, and they would keep him safe. "I'm still scared," said the boy. So the mother began to talk to him about Jesus. She told him Jesus was with him, that he was never alone, and that Jesus would always be with him. "I know Jesus is with me," said the boy, "but right now what I need is a Jesus with some skin on."

Long ago, there was an argument in heaven. Things on earth had not been going well for some time. Wars increased, poverty grew, people were selfish and leaders greedy. Rumors abounded in heaven that God had a plan to do something about it all. And every angel had an opinion about what exactly should be done.

Discussions in heavenly rooms revolved around nothing else. Angel Matthew felt that it was time for a good old fashioned, fire and brimstone sort of appearance on God's part. "Teach them a lesson," he said. "Those humans, they don't listen to much at all. They need something big! I mean, look how many prophets God has sent them over the years – maybe a dozen? They didn't pay any attention. I don't know why God didn't do this long ago. They need some good old fashioned fear of the Lord stuff, you know? Something to make 'em sit up and pay attention for once. Show 'em the word of the Lord isn't to be messed around with. Get 'em back to the ten commandments. About time, if you ask me."

"Now, Matthew," said Angel Deborah, "you know God tried that sort of approach with the flood and it didn't work at all. Sure, there was a pause in the violence for a while, but as soon as the next generations grew up, it got as bad as it ever was. Worse, even! What those people need is a good teacher, a good moral example. Someone to explain things to them. You're right about the ten commandments; maybe they just don't understand them very well. If someone could just explain to them why God wants them to act this way, I'm sure they'd do it."

"You're both way off base," said Angel Terence. And the argument began. The halls of heaven echoed with angel opinions about what God should do. Off in the corner, Angel Isaac thought privately that the fire and brimstone set was onto something. Surely God needed to do something big. Something dramatic. Isaac had been watching the humans for a while, and they didn't seem to pay much attention to each other, much less to God. But Isaac was sure God would know what to do.

Then the rumors began, and the angels argued even more. Word had it that the plan involved a baby, a virgin, a manger, and a road trip to some nothing little town called "Bethlehem." Isaac felt sure the rumors must be wrong when he heard them first. Surely God wouldn't think of a plan as ridiculous as that? It must be a PR trick to throw them off base. But day after day, week after week, the rumors persisted so much that Isaac began to worry they were true. What could God be thinking? Could God possibly be making a mistake? Isaac wasn't sure he wanted to accuse God of this. But he worried. He paced back and forth on the golden streets. Something had to be done. Finally, he headed out for the heavenly throne room. He thought long and hard about what he might say to the Almighty, and as he walked he practiced it, head down, walking as quickly as possible until he turned a corner and ran straight into...

"God!" said Isaac.
"Yes?" said God.
"I was just coming to see you," said Isaac.

"I thought you might be," said God.

"Oh, good," said Isaac. "Listen, I've been hearing some..."

"Rumors?" asked God.

"Yes," said Isaac with relief, "rumors. Right. And I have some, well, I've got a few, you know..."

"Concerns," said God.

"Yes," said Isaac. "Right. Concerns. I have some concerns. I have one concern. It's about this, um, well, I've heard there might be a..."

"Baby," said God.

"Yes! That's funny," said Isaac. "You're good at this."

"It's like I'm God," said God.

"Right," said Isaac, blushing with embarrassment. "I'm just wondering if a baby is really the way to go. You know, those people down there have babies all the time. I don't think they're going to pay much attention to another one. I think what you want is something bigger."

"Bigger?" asked God.

"Right," said Isaac. "Bigger. More dramatic. More..."

"God-like?" asked God.

"Right!" said Isaac. "Exactly. More God-like."

"Alright," said God. "What would you think would be God-like?"

"Well," said Isaac, flattered to be asked, "something dramatic, you know, maybe with angels and fire and lightening, maybe a little brimstone if you want, but if that's too much for you, just something really big. Something that announces your presence, you know? You want something to make them really pay attention to you. Listen to you. That way they'll know what you're really about."

"Ah," said God. "Interesting."

Isaac began to get worried. "But God, don't you understand? They don't listen. They don't listen to anybody, and not even to you. You need to convince them. And you need something big to do it."

"Maybe," said God.

Then Isaac thought about something else. "Also, God," he said, "I'm concerned about security issues. Have you thought about that?"

"Security issues?" asked God.

"Yes," said Isaac. "From what I can tell, babies are not very good at defending themselves. They can't even sit up, did you know that? I mean, people could do anything they wanted to you if you were a baby."

"I suppose so," said God.

"Yes," said Isaac, realizing that he was on a roll. "They could hurt you. Or stop feeding you. Or leave you outside in the cold. If you're so insistent on the baby thing, could you at least take some security precautions? Maybe you could be a magical baby."

"Magical?" asked God.

"It wouldn't take much," Isaac said quickly. "All you'd need is something like the power to be invisible, or run really fast, or maybe the ability to hurl bolts of lightning, you know, just in case. Something simple."

"Interesting," said God. "Any other suggestions?"

"I'm just worried about the risk," said Isaac sadly. "I know you love the people. I love them too. But you could really get hurt, doing this."

"Yes," said God.

And then God thanked Isaac for his concern. It turned out that several other angels had come to God already with similar ideas, including the suggestion that he should skip the baby phase and come straight into the world as a grown-up, and also the idea that he should have some serious martial arts skills.

But God, after thanking all the angels for their creativity, said no, he thought he would just be a regular baby.[1]

---

[1] Inspired by Barbara Brown Taylor, "God's Daring Plan," <u>Bread of Angels</u>. Pgs. 31-35.

"You can't make anyone love you, Isaac," said God. "Love never comes from fear. I can't make them love each other. I can't even make them love me, because love cannot be forced. Even by me. Love is a gift, and they need to learn about gifts."

"So you're giving them a baby," said Isaac.

"Yes," said God. "And perhaps they will begin to listen, and learn. There are three important things to remember in life, Isaac: faith, hope, and love. And the greatest of these is love."

"That's good," said Isaac. "Someone should write that down."

"Someone probably will," said God. "But for now, I will choose to come to them as a baby."

"God as a baby," said Isaac. "Are you sure you don't want any magical powers?"

"Yes," said God.

"Will you fit in the manger?"

"Yes," said God.

"So you'll be just like them."

"Yes," said God.

"God as a baby," Isaac said slowly.

"Yes," said God.

Isaac smiled. "God with skin on."

"Yes," smiled God.

And the Word became flesh and dwelled among us, and we have seen his glory, as of a Father's only Son, filled with grace and truth.

The Trouble with God
by Beverly Berg

The animal graveyard was a quiet place on a knoll that was shaded by two large cottonwood trees. The animals who were buried there had lived and had been loved by me for a long time; but they died and had to be buried. The winter was the worst time, because the snow covered the graves then. And when the large flakes started fallin' on the dried-up flowers and small wooden crosses that I had placed on the graves—well, there didn't seem to be any God at all then. I was sure of that. But sometimes in the spring, I'd think that there might be a God when the green grass came up through the snow. When the snow started to cover the crosses, I'd just sit there and watch; and when they were all covered and the snow looked wavy like white water and I couldn't see the graves any more, I'd miss my animals all the more because I couldn't see the graves. And the moon made little silver dots all over the snow, and they glistened like diamonds; but they were cold—not warm—like the heartbeat of my animals when they were alive. And then I'd blame God.

My pony was buried in one of the graves. He was black with white legs and had a small circle of white on his left rear. I had loved him for a long time, but he died. Pete, the sheepherder, had helped me dig the grave.

Pete had one leg cut off short and had white hair and deep wrinkles in his sun-tanned face. When he laughed, he put his head back and laughed loud. He had a different kind of a laugh, not just an ordinary one like other people. It was hard for him to dig because he had to put his stump of a leg in the crutch and balance himself while he dug.

My pet antelope was buried there, too. I remember when my dad brought him home, just lyin' there right in front of him in the saddle. He was a tiny baby whose mother had died and I raised him on a bottle. He was really big when he died. And if it hadn't been for that dang coyote, he'd be alive yet! I'll bet he followed me around for a million miles.

The snow was fallin' hard and fast now; and if you looked up into the sky, you could see millions and millions of flakes comin' down in the moonlight. They seemed like a magic curtain all around me and my graveyard. People said if you prayed, you'd feel better about things; but I tried and it never worked. The animals were still dead, and I still felt the same. Most of my soul was buried with the animals under the snow. I only had a little piece left because I had to give the animals most of it so they'd have one; because people said they didn't have souls. And Noah, he was a dang fool to try and get all of those animals in that boat; any fool would know better than to pull a dumb thing like that. I had to find out though—if there was a God. One day I got my chance.

It was early summer when Pete rode in from his sheep herdin'. It was funny to see his crutch bouncin' up and down where it was tied to the back of the saddle. It kept bouncin' and keepin' time to the rhythm of his horse Colonel's hoofbeats. I always wanted to ask Old Pete where his other leg was, but never could because I thought he might have it buried somewhere. I thought it might be a private matter with him, like my secrets, and not to be discussed. I figured if he'd 'uv' wanted me to know, he'd 'uv' told me.

He said he had to ride into town to get some supplies. I knew he wanted me to watch the sheep while he was gone. He said his sheep wagon was at the foot of the Missouri where the badlands come in close, but was far enough away from them so the sheep wouldn't wander in between them and get nabbed by a coyote. He said he'd lost one lamb yesterday. "One of those dang coyotes," he'd said.

I liked it when he said "dang"—he said it good, like he really hated those coyotes! He did everything good though, like rollin' cigarettes. He could just whip that Bull Durham out of his pocket and like a flash roll a cigarette with one hand. And the way he could strike a match on the seat of his pants was really somethin' to see. I liked to see his tongue, too, when he'd lick the paper to glue the cigarette together. It was the reddest tongue you ever saw! I loved Pete; I really did love him. When he'd pet me on the hand, I felt warm all over. I said that I'd get ready right away. Pete said that he'd be back the next day, but I knew he'd get drunk when he was in town and wouldn't be back until the day after he thought he would. And when he came back he'd always have a candy bar or some Cracker Jack for me. I liked the Cracker Jack the best because it always had a prize in it. I hoped he'd stay and get drunk so I'd have time to find out about God.

My dad saddled up Old Paint while I went to the house to get my supplies together. I filled my canteen at the artesian well, put everything in a gunny sack and tied it, along with my boots, onto the back of the saddle. Old Paint seemed ready to go. I could tell by the way he'd try to pull the reins out of my hands. I put my bare feet into the stirrup and lifted my small body into the saddle. My dad walked over close to me and said that there was kerosene in the lantern at the wagon, and to watch out for rattlers. I noticed he was lookin' at my gunny sack, and I hoped he din't see the outline of the Bible in there because I'd swiped it from the kitchen. I figured I'd have to have it to find out about God. I reached into my pocket to feel and make sure my knife hadn't fallen through a hole in my pocket, because I'd need that too, to find out.

It was a long way to the wagon, along the winding Missouri River and through the buffalo berry bushes. The berries were still green, but they were growing pretty big, and they were a beautiful green because they were next to those small grey leaves. I'd be glad when they turned red though, so I could eat them. I liked them, but they were sour and always made spit come under my tongue and made my jaws ache. The leaves on the cottonwoods were still small and light green in color; and when the breeze went through them, they made a good sound. Their sound would be different when they got larger and thicker in the late summer.

The sun was directly above now and was very hot. We'd come quite a long ways already; and as we had to cross the Missouri at this spot, I thought we'd stop and rest a spell. Old Paint put his nose halfway down into the Missouri and made lots of slurping noises while he drank, and I could feel the water going into his belly as he gulped it down. I dismounted and threw the reins over his head—which meant that he could walk around and eat some grass. The draggin' rein told him to stay near. He knew because he was a Western horse, and all Western horses knew that. I loosened his cinch because it was so hot and unstrapped my gunny sack from the back of the saddle. I walked over to the edge of the river and sat on the bank putting my feet down into the water so the Missouri could run over them. That was a good thing in life—puttin' my hot feet in the Missouri. I took my water flask out of the gunny sack and gulped some—like the way the water sounded when it hit the bottom of my stomach; but it wasn't as loud as when old Paint did it.

The smells were good here too; and the meadowlarks kept singin'. Their song was the best sound of all the spring sounds. They made you forget the sound of the coyote at night. I hated their coyote sound because it always reminded me of the graves. I took some of Mom's homemade bread and some cheese out of the sack and began to eat. I took the Bible out of the bag and stretched, so I could reach a rock that rose up out of the Missouri, and placed the Bible on the rock. The top part of the rock was dry, so the Bible wouldn't get wet. It was so hot that I moved my seat down into the water by pressing my heels down into the sandy bottom and bringin' the rest of me closer to my feet. The water was up to my waist now. I sat eatin' my bread and cheese and watched the leaves and twigs float by in the Missouri. The Bible just sat there on the rock defyin' me, and the water made a bubbly sound as it went around the rock. I finished my bread and cheese and washed it down with a gulp from the Missouri.

I stood up and walked over to the Bible and felt my jackknife in my pocket. I lifted my foot to kick the Bible into the Missouri and let old Noah "drown" along with the rest of the stories. And it could just set there on the bottom of the Missouri and not bother people any more with its foolishness! But there were more Bibles, so what was the use.

I picked it up and opened it to where the marker was. If the Angel didn't come and stop me, then I'd know there was no God. I'd know for sure. But if the Angel did come and stop me, then I'd know there was a God. I'd know that I'd see my animals again, and that it was all right for winter to come and cover up the graves with snow. I'd know for sure that the pieces of my soul that were in the graves with the animals weren't wasted there. It was awful to think about those pieces just lyin' there goin' to waste because I hardly had any soul left now. Maybe I didn't have enough left to get to heaven—if there was one.

I snapped the Bible shut and walked out of the Missouri. But I felt sick when I felt the sharp knife in my pocket, and the cheese came up in my throat, and I had to gulp it down again. And I wished I had a hankie to blow my nose. I placed the Bible and canteen back into the gunny sack and walked over to Old Paint who was switching flies with his tail. I tightened the cinch, retied my gunny sack onto the back of that saddle, reached for the reins and mounted.

As we crossed the Missouri, I noticed that the sun had moved a little and the shadows were longer. We headed into the badlands now, and I'd have to start watchin' for snakes. Old Paint was really rattlesnake shy. I'd been thrown a couple of times because I couldn't hold the saddle. The sound of the rattle made him wild. I hated that sound too. It was a sickly dead sound; and when I heard it, I felt like I did when I heard the coyote's howl. And I always felt lonely because it reminded me of the graves.

It was getting hot, and I wished I'd remembered my hat. The sun beat down on my head, and I began to feel a little dizzy. I took a towel from my sack and poured water on it from my canteen and wrapped it round my head. Old Pete told me to do that once on account of sun stroke. The sound of the sheep bells and Tippy the sheepdog's bark told me that we were almost there. We were passin' through some badlands now. They looked like huge haystacks sittin' all over, except they were mostly a dull grey. Sage brush and cactus was everywhere, and Old Paint made a swish-swishing sound with his legs as they touched the bushes when he walked through them. A few lizards hurriedly crawled under rocks when they heard us, and the meadowlarks seemed to be singin' all over. I watched the ground pretty close because I wanted to be able to "hold my saddle" if one of those dang snakes cut loose with a rattle.

Tippy's bark seemed closer now, and I hoped that he'd watched the lambs good. It was awful to see what was left of a lamb when the coyotes got a hold of him. There was only the wool and the blood left. But Tippy was a good sheepdog. I remembered my own dog buried in the graveyard, and maybe I thought he had been a better sheepdog than Tippy. I notice when somethin's dead, people always think it's better than what lives; even if it isn't. It's like my horse (the one buried in the graveyard), I can't like Old Paint as much as my other horse, no matter how hard I try, because the second time's never the same.

It was awful hot now, and I was glad to see the sheep wagon nestled under a big cottonwood. I'd forgotten that the Missouri came so close to the badlands. It was good though; I liked to be close to the Missouri and it was close for the sheep to get water.

I could see a small black dog moving toward us, and comin' fast. It was Tippy. He told us so when he started his bark. I dismounted to greet him, not botherin' with the stirrup, but just jumping to the ground. I knelt and hugged and kissed him, and he happily returned my kisses all over my face with his tongue. It was as good as seein' a real person.

My feet were still bare, and I was afraid of the diamondbacks, so I unlashed my boots from the back of the saddle, took a once-clean pair of sox from my pocket, and placed them on my dirtier feet. My thick black leather boots would protect me from the snakes, at least around the lower part of my legs. I wiggled my toes, but they still felt like they were in prison. We walked together, Tippy and I, over a small hill, while I lead Old Paint. When we reached the top of the hill, we could see the wagon again, a little less than a mile away. (I'd say, as the crow flies.)

It was really hot and dusty and hard to walk while dodgin' the sage brush and cactus. I took the canteen from the gunny sack and gulped some water. Tippy licked his lips, and I knew that he wanted some, so I held his mouth open and poured it in. Most of it spilled out because dogs drink water with their tongues, but I heard him swallow some. I poured some in my hand and held it under Old Paint's mouth. He licked my hand with his tongue. I poured the rest of the water on the towel on my head and placed the canteen back in the gunny sack.

As we neared the wagon, it began to look bigger. Funny how things look so little when they're far away. I couldn't figure why they didn't call it a covered wagon like they used to in the olden days, but nobody called it that any more. It was gittin' bigger and bigger now as we came up to it. It looked friendly, and I was glad to get to it. I wondered why I'd never named it.

I was tired and hot, but I looked around to see if I could see a good place to find out about God, because that's why I'd brought the Bible and that's why I had sharpened my knife on the sharpening stone before I left. But I had to check the sheep first. I couldn't always think about what I wanted to do because work had to come first. I mounted Old Paint and 'loped down to the sheep. They were a little ways off from the badlands, and the grass looked good, and I didn't see any signs of lost lambs. Tippy had done a good job, and I told him what a good dog he was. I turned Old Paint around to head back to the wagon, leaning my body forward in the saddle, and he knew I meant go, and go fast. I had a lot to do and important things on my mind that had to be settled once and for all.

A barrel filled with water was sitting in the shade next to the wagon. I removed the lid and found a dipper sitting on the wagon tongue. I dipped water from the barrel and poured it over my head. It really felt good running down over my body. Water was one of the good things in life, especially if a body was thirsty or hot. I wished I had time to take a swim in the Missouri, but I had too much work to do to find out about God. I dumped water in a bucket for Tippy and Paint to drink because we'd have to wait until tomorrow to go to the river for a swim.

It was getting late now; the sun was three-quarters of the way across the sky and the shadows were different. I removed Old Paint's saddle and bridle and staked him with his halter rope to the old cottonwood. He just stood there with his eyes closed, switching flies with his tail. Tippy lay next to him, panting from the heat and making huffing sounds as his tongue moved with each pant.

It was time now to begin my work. I needed rocks, and lots of them, because I had to build it just like the picture in the Bible. There are always plenty of rocks around when you don't want them; but when you want them, you can never find them. And when you do find them, they are always stuck in the ground. But then—lots of things are like that. The sun was farther down in the sky, and the shadows changed again. I had a pretty big pile of rocks now, almost as big as the altar in the picture in the Bible.

But the sun had been too hot, and the day had been too long and I began to feel dizzy. I walked over to the cottonwood and curled up beside Tippy and fell asleep.

When I awoke, the other half of the sun was just settin' behind a badland; and I knew it would be dark soon. I was kind of relieved that it was getting' dark, and I could put off God until tomorrow. It was too dark for the angel to see me anyway—that is, if there was an angel like the story in the Bible said. Maybe that story was a darned lie. I'd be in real trouble if it was. But people said you was supposed to believe everything the Bible said. Those people sure don't know anything about mixin' animals up. That must have been a real noisy ark for Noah with all them animals fightin'. He must really have been crazy to try a darn fool stunt like that! Nobody could be that dumb! I hope there was a Noah, though. "I hope so," I said, as I looked over at the altar. It looked like one big rock now, because it was so dark.

I had been so busy I had forgotten that I hadn't even been in the wagon. I grabbed my gunny sack off the ground and moved up the large wagon tongue. Tippy followed me into the wagon. It was dark now, and I groped my way around the small room, feelin' for matches. The moon streamed into the wagon and gave me some light to find the matches and light the lantern. The light, although dim, made me feel better. I was glad it was lit because the coyotes were startin' to howl, and they sounded awful close. I just sat on Pete's bed with Tippy for a while because I felt so lonely. I always felt lonely when the coyotes howled. I lit a fire in Pete's small black stove and the fire looked friendly and sounded good when the wood cracked, and the color was pretty. But when I went to cut Pete's slab of bacon with my knife, I really got the shakes at the sight of that knife! I breathed heavily and felt sick when I thought of what I had to do with it to find out about God. But I was hungry, so I laid the bacon in Pete's big black fryin' pan and it began to sizzle. I took from my gunny sack some bread and cheese which completed the supper for Tippy and me.

I took the lantern and Tippy, and brought some oats to Old Paint. We walked over to check the sheep, but they were in close to the wagon, all huddled together for the night, and we didn't see any sign of trouble. On the way back to the wagon we stopped in front of the rock altar. I began to hate it; but it drew me to it. I knew I couldn't back down now because I'd never get another chance like this, and everything was ready for tomorrow.

But later, as Tippy and I lay in Pete's bed, I wished that tomorrow would never come. But it did come, and fast, too. The sun streamed into the small opening at the side of the bed, and the dust particles danced in the light. I'd slept in my clothes, so all I had to do was put my boots on. Tippy was gone, but I knew he'd gone to check on the sheep because the door was open and I knew he'd nosed it open.

I looked outside through Pete's door and saw the rest of the sun come up. It was cool and the meadowlarks was singin', and the pile of rocks was sittin' there just starin' back. I knew it was time now to find out about God. I took the Bible from the gunny sack and opened it to "the place." But when I took the Bible to the rock altar, I couldn't feel anything. I touched my face, but it was like my fingers never touched it at all. My legs moved toward the sheep like a river runs, not with any feelin' that it's runnin'—it just runs.

I grabbed a lamb, and it bleated and tried to get away. I couldn't remember walkin' back to the rocks with the lamb, but all of a sudden I was there, like sometimes when you dream you're floatin'. But maybe it was a sign that God was comin'. Tippy was beside me, and I heard his tail waggin' against the rocks. It was the only sound I heard because the meadowlarks stopped singin' and there wasn't any sheep bells ringin'—just no sound at all.

I placed the lamb in the center of the altar and held it down with my left knee and hand. I reached into my pocket for my pocket knife—but somehow it felt different. My head didn't seem to be connected to me. My hand brought the knife slowly from my pocket and stuck it between my teeth, clawing at the blade with its fingers trying to release the blade from its folds in the knife. As the blade was released, I grasped the knife with a firm grip on the handle; and the blade glistened in the sunlight as it hung straight down. With a quick upward motion, my arm shot toward the skies while my hand had a death-like grip on the sharp knife.

And then I spoke to God. "God, if you're up there, please send one of your angels to stop me from killin' and sacrificin' this lamb—like you stopped Abraham from killin' his son Isaac. And if you don't stop me, I'll know that all of your stories are nothin' but a pack of lies."

I looked around for the angel—just prayin' that there'd be one—but there wasn't any. I couldn't give up hope though; maybe he just couldn't find me. My arm was getting' tired up there like that, and the lamb was hard to hold down. My whole body began to sob, and I wished that angel would hurry up and come! I took another firm grip on the knife, and the small muscle in my right upper arm tightened. I could scarcely breathe now, and my heartbeats sounded in my ears. "Please come, angel, please come, I don't want to kill this lamb," I said. I knew if I went this far, God would really be mad if I didn't sacrifice the lamb.

And then I heard it—that quick short sickening sound. The sound of the diamondback. I froze. The lamb bounded away. I turned as a panther would turn—trying desperately to spot him. If he was within striking distance of me, I knew that one quick move would be all I'd have to make. Again, the death rattle filled the still morning with all the hate of the world wrapped up in one sound. Old Paint reared and snorted and pawed the ground like an angry bull. I spotted him then, not a dozen feet away from Old Paint. Tippy stayed at my side in a crouched position, his lips curled up in a growl and showing his long fangs. I moved with cat-like motion to the tongue of the wagon and went up to the wagon like a skilled tight-rope walker. I knew Pete's gun was behind the stove, and I knew it was loaded. I couldn't get an aim from the door of the wagon, as Old Paint had shifted his position and was between the snake and me. I moved quickly back down the tongue, gripping the large heavy gun in both hands. I talked quietly to the animals, trying to quiet them down so as not to disturb the snake. But old Paint was rilin' him with his stompin and snortin', and he rattled and coiled. And I aimed and fired.

I heard a meadowlark. And the dust blew away. It was still movin' its dead body back and forth, but snakes and chickens always moved, even after they were dead. I never could figure that out. I took Pete's shovel and buried it right where it lay. Paint moved up to me and rubbed his face on my body, and I threw my arms around his neck and cried on his shoulder. Tippy jumped on me and licked my face.

I moved over to the rock altar and set on it for a long time—thinkin'. It was the gun that puzzled me. I just couldn't remember pullin' the trigger. I couldn't remember cockin' it either. Maybe when I closed my eyes, the Angel did it; maybe that's what happened. It seemed like the meadowlarks was singin' all over, and I saw that the Bible still lay open on the altar.

INDEX of Author's Names, First Lines and illustrations

A mother crept into her young son's room, 101
After a year of living in an apartment, 78
Anderson, Patricia, xii, 98
Arriving home after a long day, 24
As my hand reached for the bread, 28
At the shoreline, 52
Attitude is everything, 68
Berg, Beverly, xii, 16, 38, 41, 45, 106
Berries? Go berries?" I loved to go berry-picking, 88
Brask, Minna, xii, 77, 78
Brask, Otto, xiii, 7, 58
Dear God, my daily guide throughout my life, 18
Deskin, Kim, xiii, 8, 10, 64
Early one May morning, 60
Easter morning, we all go to church, 8
Friend, I'm grateful for the days we share, 91
Halfway through preparing my weekly, 31

Hanley, Clara, xiii, 11
Hanley, Ruth, xiv, 12, 54, 76, 86, 87
Honey, the Easter Bunny is coming, 76
I complain about, 57
I have carried a piece of you since my beginning, 54
I live in a part of the country, now, 64
I love to travel! I love the adventure, 4
illustration, 2, 4, 8, 19, 52, 60, 69, 78, 89, 93
It was a big old white house on the corner, 80
It was my father's birthday, 77
Jacobsen, Lyla, xiv
Mason, Pat, xv, 52, 53, 63
McCallum Sachse, Pastor Katy, xiv, 101
mmm it's sweet" says Mom, 87
Morris, Pastor Larry, xv, 2, 26, 30, 49, 70, 80, 92, 94

Morris, Suzanne, xv, 19, 20, 56
My father's hat hung on a nail, 38
Negativity kills, 72
No one would have guessed my cousin Bob could, 98
Now I lay me down to sleep', 12
Obie, Marlene, xv, 18, 48, 55, 57, 66, 68, 72
Oh, no! Tami! I forgot to bring my sandals!, 14
On a sunny day, a few days before Easter, 7
On my way to the Sudoku, 84
Once upon a time, 36, 70
Patneaude, David, xvi, 84
Remember you are dust, 30
Rhythmic breathing and lazy suck of the pacifier, 86
She had been a pastor, 26
Sometimes you find the hand of God, 58
Stars, 22
Taylor, Ross, xvi
The animal graveyard was a quiet place, 106
The calendar that hung on a nail, 45

The four of us, my older sister Jean, 16
The ground, the earth, dirt, acreage, the fields, 49
The light is increasing yet remains elusive, 53
The prison in Illinois where I worked, 41
The sound of a plane overhead, 19
The water runs over the head, 2
There are qualities in a blade of grass, 20
There was a man, 10
They enter softly and slowly, 55
They still sell boxes of 32 tiny valentines, 92
Time drags, that's a gift, 66
To smell a forest, 56
Water is not what it appears to be, 63
We are the girls, 11
When the ceiling above you is falling down, 94
Why did she not cry, 48
Wilson, RuthAnn, xvi, 4, 14, 22, 24, 28, 31, 36, 60, 88, 91

Made in the USA
Charleston, SC
20 October 2011